SECRETS
OF A
MILLIONAIRE
REAL ESTATE
INVESTOR

ROBERT SHEMIN, ESQ.

DEARBORN™
TRADE
A **Kaplan Professional** Company

Acquisitions Editor: Mary B. Good
Senior Managing Editor: Jack Kiburz
Interior Design: Lucy Jenkins
Cover Design: Design Alliance, Inc.
Typesetting: Elizabeth Pitts

Library of Congress Cataloging-in-Publication Data

Shemin, Robert, 1963-
    Secrets of a millionaire real estate investor / Robert Shemin.
       p.   cm.
Includes index.
    ISBN 0-7931-3705-5 (pbk.)
    1. Real estate investment.   I. Title.
    HD1382.5 .S53   2000
    332.63'24--dc21

                                                    00-009301

Dearborn books are available at special quantity discounts to use as premiums and sales promotions, or for use in corporate training programs. For more information, please call the Special Sales Manager at 800-621-9621, ext. 4514, or write to Dearborn Financial Publishing, Inc., 155 North Wacker Drive, Chicago, IL 60606-1719.

Dedication

To Patricia and Alexander. Thank you for all of your love and support.

CONTENTS

ACKNOWLEDGMENTS

Thank you to all the good people at Dearborn who helped this book be published: to my editor Mary B. Good; to Annc Basye for her developmental editorial assistance; to Ray Binion, Hal Wilson, Tommy Tow, and the real estate associations around the United States for helping me in real estate; and to my parents for their support.

INTRODUCTION

Your Foundation for Financial Independence

Money makes money; and the money money makes, makes more money.

–Ben Franklin

Investing in real estate always has been—and always will be—one of the best methods for making money and accumulating wealth. Your largest financial asset is probably your home. You may know someone who bought a home and sold it a few years later for a substantial profit. Perhaps your parents or grandparents paid $35,000 for a home that is now worth $350,000 or more.

Real estate appreciates because its quantity is limited, and, as this book will show you, it's possible to buy real estate at a substantial discount. Many houses valued at $100,000 can be bought for $75,000. This is unlike stock, which is an investment that always must be purchased at full market value; that is, you buy it for $75 a share in hopes that it goes to $100. Real estate investors buy property for less than it is worth every day, and so can you.

Simply speaking, you have only two things to invest: your time and your money. Investing in stocks or bonds generally takes cash, while investing in real estate doesn't always require money. You can buy real estate with little or no credit or cash, perhaps borrowing all of the money from a lender or seller, or by transferring title to a buyer seeking a good deal.

Real estate investing does take time—time to learn how to find an undervalued property and time to prepare it for resale at its full value. It also takes time to identify good rental properties. But the rewards are great. When you buy a house valued at $100,000 for $75,000, you'll see your net worth immediately increase by $25,000! The gain can be immediate if you are able to turn around and sell it to another party; or it can be long term if you become a landlord. As a landlord, you can depreciate and write off of your taxes ⅟₂₈ of the value of your property every year, along with loan interest and most repairs, taxes, and insurance. If you buy a property at a good price, the rent should cover your costs for your loan payment, repairs, taxes, and insurance. Thus, over time your tenants pay down your debt, while the value of your property typically increases. In many cases, you can earn a positive cash flow on a rental property, yet not be taxed on it.

Real Estate Can Make You a Millionaire

Imagine for a moment that after reading this book you find a two-unit duplex valued at $100,000 for $75,000. You borrow the $75,000, based on the value of the property and not on your credit, to buy it from a bank or private lender or you get the seller to provide financing. Then, you rent the duplex for $650 per month per unit.

Let's do the math: The property is worth $100,000. Your loan and purchase price is $75,000. Your net worth goes up $25,000. Your rental income for two units at $650 each equals $1,300 per month, which covers the $800 monthly payment on a 20-year, 9 percent, $75,000 loan.

If you make a $100 profit each month, the return on your investment is not 10 percent, not 30 percent, but an infinite return, because none of your money is invested in the property. If your interest rate is fixed, your loan payment has stayed the same, and your rent has increased every couple of years, 20 years from now the tenants will have paid off your debt. The value of your property probably also will rise, perhaps even doubling or tripling to $200,000 or $300,000. If you could find and buy one property like this every year for 6 years, 20 years from now your six properties, debt free, would be worth at least $1,200,000—and still be generating rental income!

So over time—and with work—real estate can make you a millionaire. You can develop tremendous wealth with real estate, and you also can create a lifetime income that is paid whether you are working or not. The rent money just keeps coming!

If It Works Once, Why Not Do It Again!

You probably know someone who has made a lot of money buying and selling a house. My challenge to you is: *If it works once, why not do it again?* With just a little knowledge, desire, and effort, part-time or full-time, you can make a lot of money in real estate. The first deal is always the hardest, so get started now. Once you learn the concepts I'm about to show you—and apply them step by step—it becomes easier and easier. Wherever you are, there is always a good deal to be found—and room for another educated, persistent real estate investor. You can and will be successful if you want to be!

So do a deal. Make a good profit and do it again and again. Happy investing!

Turning Properties into Profits

The winners in life think constantly in terms of I can, I will, and I am. Losers, on the other hand, concentrate their waking thoughts on what they should have or would have done, or what they can't do.

–Dr. Dennis Waitley

I was a financial consultant with no interest in real estate investing–and absolutely no desire to start investing–the day I called on a sweet old couple in a small town near Nashville. These people were as kind as could be, but I was sure that calling me was a mistake. At the time, I only worked with people who had $3 to $5 million to invest, and I was positive that this modest couple didn't make the grade. Then the man invited me to take a look at his books.

I was astonished. He owned 120 houses, every one of them paid for–and each one bought for about 50 cents on the dollar. Close to $70,000 in rental income arrived every month, and he and his wife spent six months a year on vacation.

Well, that got me hooked. In the months to come, I interviewed 100 investors and 200 tenants to try to learn the secrets of real estate investing. I made a business plan, set goals, and began looking at houses. Two hundred properties later, I hadn't yet made an offer. I was still scared, and I was sure I didn't know enough. Finally after six months of searching, I bought my first rental property.

That was in 1991. Since then, I've acquired more than 200 pieces of real estate worth more than $10 million. I've also been involved in more than 600 real estate transactions, and I manage more than 200 houses and duplex units in Nashville, Tennessee.

My experience has taught me that there are basically three strategies for making money in real estate:

1. Buying and "flipping" the property, ideally before closing, to another buyer (another investor or someone who will live in the property) for more money
2. Buying, rehabbing, and reselling the property
3. Buying and holding the property as a landlord

If you have money, all three strategies are open to you, and your choice will depend on the type of return you want in relation to your risk tolerance. If you have little or no cash, you still can pursue these strategies, but you will need to be more creative about financing. You will want to buy property with little (or no) money out of your own pocket. You can flip and lease-option properties, which require little or no cash or credit. You might try to assume the existing loan on the property, or ask the seller for owner's terms. You even can try to partner the deal with the seller by offering to fix up the property and sell it for a share of the profits over and above a fixed price. If you have to borrow the money, offer friends and family a first mortgage and a higher rate of return than they can get on their money elsewhere. You also can try to partner a deal with a contractor or handyman who will do the work and split the profits with you, or partner a deal with a friend or a relative.

Let's examine the three major money-making strategies more closely.

Buying and Flipping

If you find a 1999 Mercedes convertible sports coupe in good condition that you can buy for $18,000 (a new one sells for $75,000+), do you think you can sell it and make a profit? Of course!

If you find a house or piece of land worth $50,000 that you can buy for $25,000, or a duplex worth $200,000 that you can buy for $100,000, do you think you can make money? You bet!

Finding an undervalued property, putting it under contract, and immediately reselling it to another buyer is called "flipping" the property. You never own the property, so you never have to put down money or borrow it. You find the property and sell the right to purchase it to someone else. Flipping can be very lucrative. One investor in my town makes more money than most bank presidents and law partners simply by finding good deals, putting them under contract, and assigning or selling the contracts to other investors. An attorney does all the paperwork so the investor can spend his time finding good deals. If for some reason the buyer or assignee of the contract does not close, the investor can legally and ethically keep the money that he was paid by the buyer or assignee for the option to buy it. Furthermore, because he has a contingency clause in all of his contracts, he is not obligated to close or buy the house.

To buy and flip a property, find a home that you know is undervalued and whose seller is motivated. Suppose you know that the house should be valued at $80,000, but the seller is selling it for $60,000 and you negotiate the seller down to $50,000 cash. You now have two options:

1. Contract to buy the home for $50,000 to close in 45 days. Make sure both you and the seller sign. *Be sure to include a contingency clause so you can get out of the deal if it goes sour!* (See Chapter 5 for sample contingency clauses.)
2. Sign a 45-day option to buy the property for $50,000 cash. Again, make sure both you and the seller sign.

Technically speaking, there is little difference between a contract with a contingency clause and an option to buy. Both will allow you to walk away from a deal if you discover, while analyzing the property, that it is not a good deal. And whether you sign a contract or an option, be sure to protect yourself by recording it at the recorder of deeds or courthouse.

Once you control the property, you need to find a buyer—quickly! Chapter 2 will show you how to build a network of investors, buyers, property owners, and agents interested in buying property. Tell everyone in the network that they can buy a house valued at $80,000 for much less—$65,000—but must do so within 30 days. If you found a good deal, there is no doubt another investor is willing to buy the house from you for the right price.

When you find your buyer, you assign your contract—basically, your right to buy the house—for $15,000 (the difference between your contract purchase price and the price you are selling it for). By assigning the contract, you're allowing the new buyer to step into your shoes. The new buyer will purchase the house from the original seller for $50,000 and pay you $15,000 for the right to purchase the house for $50,000. You make $15,000. Here's the math:

Value of house:	$80,000
You agree to pay seller:	$50,000
Your buyer pays:	$65,000
You make:	$65,000 – $50,000 = $15,000

You sign a contract with the new buyer to sell the house for $65,000. At the closing, you have what is known as a collapsed closing. Your buyer comes in at 2:00 PM and gives the closing attorneys (or title company) $65,000 to buy the property. At 2:30 PM, the original seller comes in, signs the deed, and collects a check for $50,000. You get a check for $15,000. The title passes from the original seller to the ultimate buyer.

It sounds fantastic—but it happens every day. You can make a profit of $500, $1,000, $5,000, or $15,000. When I buy and flip a house, I make anywhere from $2,000 to $15,000. Large deals, such as apartment buildings, land, or office buildings, can make much more—tens or even hundreds of thousands of dollars and more!

Many investors generate cash and monthly income by taking back a second mortgage as their "commission" on a buy-and-flip transaction. For example, if I buy a $150,000 property for $100,000 and sell it for $120,000, I may ask my buyer for $20,000 cash and $50 a month for 20 years. The buyer is still getting a terrific deal. Likewise, on a $100,000 rental property that I buy for $50,000 and sell for $60,000, a $50 or $100 monthly fee for a certain time period should not be a problem for the buyer. He or she is getting a great deal *and* rental income. Of course, this kind of transaction is part of the deal you negotiate and is spelled out in the contract. Like any mortgage, the note is recorded as a lien against the property so that even if the buyer defaults, you will be paid when the property is sold.

Another way to buy and flip without putting any money down is to option the property and then sell the option. An *option* is the right, not the obligation, to buy something. Options are bought and sold every day on real estate and stocks and commodities of all kinds. Many large commercial properties are bought and sold by optioning them. If you do not close or exercise your option to buy, you lose only your option money.

It works like this: When I find a $150,000 house that I can buy for $100,000, I sign an option to buy the property and sell the option to another investor for $20,000. I disclose what I am doing to both parties and sign options with each one. I am paid without having to worry about title, liability, or closing.

Some real estate investors only use options because they offer limited liability—you are not obligated to close and you keep your option money once someone buys it from you, regardless of whether they closed or exercised their option. For more information about options, visit my Web site <www.shemin.com>. I try to option at a good price as much property as I can, for as long as I can.

Is Buying and Flipping Fraudulent?

Some unsavory real estate deals designed to secure fraudulent mortgages have caused several states to pass laws that *seem* to prohibit buying and flipping. According to Peter G. Miller of *Realty Times,* flipping becomes illegal when the resale relies on inflated appraisals, fake documents, sales to straw buyers who represent original sellers, and phantom second loans. In some cases, the title on a property is moved back and forth among a group of insiders who seek to raise the sales price and create a basis for larger loans.

Illegal flipping is only a fraction of all real estate purchases—and it isn't practiced by investors who seek to make real profits on a bona fide sale to another party. Still, to make sure you don't run afoul of fraud laws, be sure to disclose what you are doing in writing to the ultimate purchaser. (See the sample disclosure form in Appendix C.) As always, it is best to check with your attorney on this.

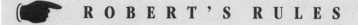

ROBERT'S RULES

When you buy and flip, don't be greedy! If you know you've found a great deal, sell it quickly for a medium to high profit. Don't try to get a big payoff. You're more likely to get a reputation as one who tries to overprice deals, which is not a reputation you want because nobody will want to do business with you. Instead of treating each flip as a one-time shot, make friends in the business by letting others profit as well. Remember, pigs get fat, hogs get slaughtered! In other words, don't be greedy.

Buying, Rehabbing, and Selling

Suppose you don't like flipping or don't think you can make much money on a property in its present condition. Still, you know that with an inexpensive face-lift, it will sell for much more than you bought it for.

Buying, repairing, and selling property can be very profitable and rewarding. The key to rehabbing a property is working with a good, reliable, and inexpensive contractor (or better yet, doing the work yourself) and estimating costs as accurately as possible. Before you purchase, get precise information from contractors to establish actual costs of fixing up the house. Your goal is to buy it for at least 40 percent off retail. Holding costs—mortgage payments, taxes, insurance, utilities, and so forth—also must be estimated. And don't forget to include your time in your costs! Many rehabbers work on a property every day for six months and forget to include a salary or pay for their efforts.

Repair and holding costs, plus the price you paid for the property, should not be more than 70 to 75 percent of what you really can sell it for. I aim to net 30 percent of the retail sales price. Be conservative when you estimate the selling price. If I think a house will sell for $70,000, I discount it by 15 percent to determine whether I will profit from the sale of the home. Anything above $59,500 is pure gravy. It is always better to make more money than you expected than it is to make less!

BUYING AND FLIPPING

Advantages: Good, quick money. You don't need capital to begin.

Disadvantages: You must know buyers who have the money to purchase quickly. If you are not able to close on the properties you lock up, word will get around not to do business with you. Also, people may get upset when they learn you were a middleperson and made a lot of money. Buyers and sellers may try to walk away from the deal. In addition, on flips, rehabbing, and reselling, the IRS will consider you a dealer. These activities will be listed as a separate type of business, and you will be taxed on your profits about 15 percent beyond your regular tax rate. This is a type of self-employment tax and one you pay on any business you start or profit from. Of course, you hardly ever pay taxes unless you make money.

Buying and Holding as a Landlord

Remember that modest-looking elderly couple whose success convinced me to go into real estate? They are among the millions of people who have discovered that buying and holding real estate as a landlord is a great way to accumulate wealth in the long run. Not only do most properties appreciate in value, but you also get a great monthly cash flow, and your tenants pay off your debt!

My rule of thumb is that a single-family house should generate a cash flow of at least $150 to $300 per month, and duplexes should generate about $200 to $400 per month. Remember that your cash flow must cover loan payments, and also the costs of the occasional vacant apartment and regular maintenance and repairs. How much cash flow multifamily properties can generate depends on rent, vacancy, repair expenses, capitalization rates, and the type and size of the buildings.

BUYING, REHABBING, AND SELLING

Advantages: There is great money to be made. You can do some of the work yourself and save money. You don't have to deal with tenants. And, you're creating housing and improving an area!

Disadvantages: Ties up capital for several months to a year while you rehab and wait to sell. Contracting and rehabbing can be time-consuming and frustrating. You may have to also pay an extra 15 percent of your profits in self-employment tax.

Landlording isn't easy. Managing properties can be a real headache. Many people are better off hiring a professional property manager to run their buildings. But by following the policies and procedures outlined in Chapter 7, you can master the ins and outs of managing rental property yourself.

Most of my properties are in low- and middle-income neighborhoods, and many of my tenants participate in the federal Section 8 housing program. I find there is less competition in these housing niches than in more expensive ones. Many landlords avoid them because they hear a few well-publicized horror stories about tenant damage. Some landlords in these neighborhoods—my competitors—are irresponsible landlords who neglect their properties and take advantage of their tenants. They expect the worst tenants, and that's exactly what they attract!

Quite honestly, 99 percent of my 140-plus tenants are downright decent people. Obviously, there's an occasional rotten apple in any real estate management operation. But by keeping my property clean and in good repair, screening tenants properly, treating them decently, and rewarding them for responsible behavior, I attract good tenants. In fact, they seek me out.

> **BUYING AND HOLDING PROPERTY AS
> A LANDLORD**
>
> ---
>
> *Advantages:* A great wealth accumulator that gen-
> erates great monthly cash flow.
>
> *Disadvantages:* May need cash for down payment
> and repairs. Managing properties and tenants can be
> a headache. Your monthly cash flow is never as much
> as you think because of vacancies and repairs. Also,
> landlording can be very time-consuming.

More Ways to Make Money in Real Estate

Although it's important to devote most of your energy to finding
good deals, there are dozens of ways to make extra income while helping people. Once you're in real estate, you'll meet contractors who need
work, building owners who need contractors, buyers who need mortgages, and mortgage companies looking for business! In many in-
stances, you can receive a commission, referral fee, or finder's fee
simply for matching up two parties who need each other.

Sometimes one deal can generate several sources of profit. When I
flip a property, I may make money by helping the investor find financing. If the property needs work, I may refer the investor to a reliable contractor, who then pays me a referral fee.

Many successful real estate investors can close or broker a deal,
arrange financing, buy and sell notes, partner with other investors, manage and repair properties, or act as real estate agents. Sometimes one
investor wears all these hats; sometimes he or she brings in associates to
handle the additional services. In the long run, they develop large businesses with many profit streams that serve as one-stop shops for real
estate investors.

And the bottom line is profit. In every real estate transaction, someone will make a commission, someone will line up the mortgage, and
someone will handle the closing, all for a fee. You may as well master as
many of these skills as possible!

It took me a few years to figure out all the ways I could profit in real estate. This section will dramatically cut your learning curve by introducing them all at once. Just remember: Always tell people and disclose in writing exactly what you are doing, especially if you are filling more than one role in the transaction process. The only way a potential conflict can lead to trouble is if you fail to inform others about it. That's called fraud. Disclose everything, and you will not be accused of committing fraud.

Licenses also may be required for some of these businesses. You may need to be licensed to be a mortgage broker or originator, and you may need to operate as a general contractor in order to broker repairs. Check with your local government agency to see if licenses are required.

Lease-Optioning

Lease-optioning is an excellent way to control real estate without using any—or much—of your own money. It is also an excellent way to profit from a property that just isn't good enough for a flip, or when you don't have the down payment and want to buy and hold a property.

Here's how a lease-option works. You negotiate a long-term lease with the seller for the lowest possible monthly payment and lowest possible deposit. You also negotiate a purchase price for the property that you can exercise any time before your option period expires (which should be as long as the lease). Make sure that the lease allows you to rent or lease-purchase the property to someone else for a higher monthly rent and a higher purchase price. You now earn money every month and can profit if your lease purchaser buys the property for the higher price.

For example, you negotiate with Joe Seller to lease-purchase his house for a $200 deposit, $450 monthly rent, and a purchase price of $59,000, all good for three years. Then you turn around and lease-purchase the property to Jill Buyer for a $1,000 option, $750 monthly rent, and an option to buy the property for $65,000, all good for two years. Your profit potential is $800 up front ($1,000 option money minus your $200 deposit). You make $300 per month on the difference in the rental rate, and if Jill buys the house, you collect $6,000. The option money is not a deposit and does not have to be returned to the renters if they decide not to buy the property.

Always use separate lease and option agreements. First, if you have to evict the renter, you can go to court with the lease. If the option is attached to a part of the lease, a judge may deem the agreement to be a purchase and not rule in your favor for a timely eviction.

When you lease-option, you can have part of your rent go toward paying down the purchase price. For example, if you pay $250 per month, $50 to $100 per month (or as much as you can negotiate) can go toward reducing your purchase price.

You also can have the original seller be responsible for repairs, just as if you were renting. However, when you lease-option the property, make your lease purchaser be responsible for the first $200 to $500 worth of repairs. Simply explain to purchasers that if it is going to be their house, they may as well start taking care of it.

LEASE-OPTIONING

Advantages: Lease-optioning is a great way to control and profit in real estate without the risks of ownership and without tying up a lot of your money. You can develop a good monthly income with little headache if you're able to negotiate away the repair responsibilities. If you can clear $200 a month on every lease-option house, you can make a nice steady income. How about 10, 20, or 30 houses at $100 or $200 per month? Meanwhile, you are collecting larger deposits on option money from your lease purchaser, so you can make thousands of dollars up front. And don't forget the back end, when your tenant decides to purchase the house: Your option to buy is less than your purchaser's option price, so the difference is your profit.

Disadvantages: Because you do not actually own the property, you won't benefit from tax depreciation. Also, you must disclose the fact that you do not own the property to all prospective lease purchasers. If you don't, and for some reason you are not able to pass along clear title to the property, you may be accused of fraud.

Finding properties to lease-option. Look in your newspaper for For Rent ads to find properties to lease-option. Call the landlords/owners and ask if they would be interested in lease-purchasing the property to you. Ask them how often they have had trouble collecting the rent and guarantee (because you are a reputable person) that they will get their rent on time every month for 1, 2, 5, 10, or 20 years. Try to get them to be responsible for the first $1,000 of repairs, but assure them that you will handle all other repair problems except for capital repairs—new heaters, air conditioners, plumbing, and other long-term improvements for which they are responsible anyway. Most landlords/owners are tired of managing their properties. A lease-option is an excellent way to alleviate their problems.

You also can contact property managers and ask them to help you negotiate with the owner. Property managers get a commission every time the rent is paid. If you can guarantee that commissions continue because the monthly rent will be paid—and you handle the work—the property manager will be getting a great deal. He or she will be even happier if you offer to give them a commission if the property is sold.

Sandwich Leasing

Sandwich leasing is lease-optioning without the option to purchase. And that's why I don't recommend it.

In sandwich leasing, Joe Renter offers to rent Jill Landlord's house for $500 and then rents it to another party for $700. Owners who agree to this arrangement may be tired of managing rental property or may be long-time landlords with below-market rents. Joe Renter gets the right to sublease or re-rent the property for three to ten years (seek the longest lease possible) and discloses the arrangement to both parties, so that both owner and sublessor are aware of it. The lease specifies that like any landlord, the owner will pay for repairs to the roof, hot water heater, and so on.

In my view, there's no point to sandwich leasing. Even someone with no money to put down can negotiate an option to purchase the property, which is what I always recommend.

> ### SANDWICH LEASING
>
> ***Advantages:*** Doesn't require capital to start and yields a good monthly income.
>
> ***Disadvantages:*** You may have all the duties and liabilities of a landlord without the privilege of owning the property.

Mortgage Brokering

Mortgage brokers match institutions with money to lend to investors who want to borrow. They are paid a commission by the institutions or borrowers for each completed deal.

The demand for mortgages is continual in the real estate investing business. It's a natural sideline to what you are doing. You can broker mortgages for one large company or be an independent who brokers deals for many companies. The average brokerage commission is $1,500 to $5,000, or ½ to 3 percent of the total loan.

> ### MORTGAGE BROKERING
>
> ***Advantages:*** A great source of extra revenue.
>
> ***Disadvantages:*** You may have to be licensed. If you're selling a house and brokering a mortgage to a buyer, you may need to follow certain disclosure laws. Be sure to find out what laws apply.

A good part of my income comes from mortgage brokering. Back in the days when I was doing a lot of lease-optioning and finding deals for other investors, I referred as many as eight buyers a month to good mortgage companies. When I realized that someone else was earning a commission on each referral, I became a mortgage originator. Now when I run across an investor who wants a mortgage, I take the initial application and submit it to the mortgage company, and I get the commission! Three to five mortgages per month can mean an extra $4,000 to $7,000 each month. Even if you only write up one mortgage a year, you've earned a weekend getaway. And again, you're doing the business anyway.

Look for a good mortgage company that gives people great service and good deals. As a mortgage broker, you'll be helping the company, closing more deals because you can help buyers get financing, and making extra money. An unbeatable formula!

Tax Certificate Brokering

Some people broker stocks and bonds. Others broker tax certificates, which are sold or auctioned by the local property tax office for properties whose owners are in arrears. By purchasing a lien, an investor eventually may become the owner of the property, unless the existing owner exercises the "right of redemption" and pays off the taxes plus interest. In that case, the investor earns as much as 14 or 18 percent interest on the certificate.

TAX CERTIFICATE BROKERING

Advantages: Can be lucrative if you can find investors willing to rely on your expertise to buy tax certificates.

Disadvantages: Very competitive; deals can be hard to find. Can be complicated and liability can be high. If you don't do your homework, a deal may go bad. You may need to be licensed, and you will need to be sure that you are not violating securities laws. Check with an attorney!

As a broker, you will bid on behalf of investors at a tax auction and charge a commission or share in the profits for your work. You may need a license to act as a broker. Be sure to research the tax certificate and sale process in your area, because every municipality is different. You also need to analyze each property thoroughly to make sure it is a good deal if the property eventually becomes yours—and that you can insure the title.

Private Money Brokering

Private money brokers match investors who want money with individuals who have money to invest. Their job is to find good loans and make good matches. For example, such a broker might borrow money from one investor at 10 percent and turn around and lend to someone else for slightly more. He or she also may charge 5 or 10 percentage points of the loan amount. Thus, for a $40,000, 15-year loan at 11 percent that is lent at 13 percent with five points, the broker would earn $2,000 up front and $60 per month for the life of the loan on the 2 percent spread.

Check with your state department of banking and mortgages to find out the laws and regulations covering private money brokers.

PRIVATE MONEY BROKERING

Advantages: Can be highly lucrative, and there is a big demand for it.

Disadvantages: Lending money is always risky; some people may not pay back the investor. You need to check the credit of borrowers very thoroughly and lend conservatively, maintaining a loan-to-value ratio of 65 percent or less. (In other words, don't lend more than 65 percent of the property's value.)

Becoming a Real Estate Agent

Becoming a real estate agent has some advantages. Because you have to go through training and be licensed, you quickly learn a lot about the real estate business. You forge connections with other agents and thus may hear about some terrific opportunities. Some of the basic equipment necessary for success in business—a fax machine and a copier—and access to the Multiple Listing Service (a listing of all properties for sale by all the real estate agents in your area) come with the territory. And, you can make between 5 and 7 percent commission on any sales you make as an agent.

On the downside, you may have to split your commission with another agent, and you absolutely will have to pay your brokerage a portion, which can range from 10 to 50 percent of your commission. You risk incurring tremendous liability and must comply with strict disclosure laws, and the same office environment that provides equipment for free may limit your ability to wheel and deal your own transactions.

Not long ago, I gave up my real estate license after being an agent for many years. For me, the downside was just too great. The potential liability was intimidating. Plus, every time I talked to people I had to disclose that I was an agent, and every time I signed a contract, I had to use special forms. Finally, I realized that being an agent and being an investor are two different things. Sure, an agent makes a commission—but when I flip or lease-option a property on my own, my profit is generally much larger than any agent commission. I am happy to leave the hard work of showing properties to real estate agents.

BECOMING A REAL ESTATE AGENT

Advantages: Earn extra commission and access to knowledgeable peers, office equipment, and the Multiple Listing Service.

Disadvantages: Too much paperwork, you may not have the freedom to pursue your own deals, and the commission is smaller than what you can make buying and selling on your own.

Consulting

Consulting is a win-win situation for the experienced investor who can turn his or her knowledge into a product. Once you've gained some experience in real estate, you will probably be besieged by requests for advice from investors. Charge an hourly fee ($35 to $200 per hour) or ask for a commission or a percentage of any deal that you assist with. If you don't, you'll be giving away your knowledge for free! You also might consider holding seminars for investors, retirees, real estate firms, estates, attorneys, certified public accountants, financial planners, non-profit organizations, and government agencies.

CONSULTING

Advantages: Very little capital required and an excellent source of additional income for the experienced investor.

Disadvantages: The cost of promoting a seminar may be high. Trust me, doing real estate deals is typically much more profitable. I can make $5,000 to $8,000 flipping a property, but only carn $2,000 for a seminar that takes me two months to put together and advertise.

Managing Property

Property managers take care of property that someone else owns. In return, they receive 8 to 11 percent of the monthly rent. Depending on how the contract is written, they also may keep late fees, application fees, and renewal fees—and even be paid a commission when the property is sold (although you may need to be a real estate agent to do so). Profits come with volume, so they need to manage many properties to secure good results.

Property managers may incur a tremendous amount of liability for property that they don't even own, and liability insurance can run $800 to $2,000 annually. They also may need to be licensed.

Personally, I think it's a lot of work for very little pay, but there is one bright spot: Property managers are in the flow of deals. When landlords want to buy or sell property, they will call you.

Good deals weren't enough to keep me in the property management business, however. Managing several hundred units for myself and other managers was a nightmare. I got into real estate investing to gain more personal freedom, but once I had a business with employees, subcontractors, tenant problems, and hundreds of phone calls, my freedom went away. And it wasn't very profitable! Today, I let a professional property manager take care of my properties, although I pitch in now and then.

MANAGING PROPERTY

Advantages: If you're buying and holding property, no one will do a better job than you in keeping an eye on your property. Working for other landlords keeps you in touch with people looking for buyers and sellers. Many contractors and maintenance people are at your disposal.

Disadvantages: It's time-consuming and you are paid very little to handle a lot of small problems. Hard to provide good service and still make any money.

Forming a Maintenance Company

When I was in property management, I set up a maintenance company that was a very large profit center. We might charge $150 to fix a water heater, even though the repair cost us $100. That compensated for the low fees we charged to manage properties.

With very little capital, you can form a maintenance company that repairs, rehabilitates, or simply "makes ready" empty units for owners. You can do the labor yourself or hire a subcontractor. You can charge by the hour or by the job for painting, carpet cleaning, rehabilitation, and landscaping.

You also can be paid for referring qualified contractors to other investors. I've gotten to know lots of contractors, and I refer them frequently. Most are grateful because while they are good craftsmen, they aren't strong marketers. They pay me a referral fee or a percentage of the job—much easier than subcontracting the work myself, and I don't have to incur the tremendous liability of being a general contractor.

FORMING A MAINTENANCE COMPANY

Advantages: The markup on cleaning and repairs can be generous, making this a very profitable sideline.

Disadvantages: You may need to be licensed, secure solid liability insurance, and hire employees. It may be easier to stick with referrals only and avoid the responsibility for operating a company. Check with a local government agency or an attorney to make sure you legally and ethically can be paid for referring repair people. Again, this can be a business with a lot of headaches, overhead, and liability.

Use Creative Selling to Buy and Create Paper

When you buy and fixup or buy and flip, accept some of the purchase price in a mortgage or note, an installment deed, or a land contract. To sell a house for $110,000, for example, you could accept $10,000 down and create a note for the $100,000 balance. Besides generating profits and cash flow, a note like this is marketable. Keep it, or raise cash by selling it at a discount to note buyers, of which there are thousands (find them on my Web site <www.shemin.com>). Note buyers will help you structure the note before you close on the deal, so you can get maximum dollar amount. Keep in mind that the worse a buyer's credit and the higher the loan-to-value ratio, the less buyers will pay for the note. "Seasoned" notes—notes held by people who have paid on time for six months, two years, and so on—will obtain a higher price.

BUY AND CREATE PAPER

Advantages: Can create good monthly cash flow, especially when you sell a property on owner's terms. Also, there are few, if any, management headaches. A great way to sell property creatively.

Disadvantages: The notes generate tax liability. Check with your accountant before you buy or sell a note. The payor on the note should have decent credit. If not, you may have to sell the note at a big discount.

Setting Your Goals and Making Your Plan

Which money-making strategy is best for you depends on your personal goals and your tolerance for risk. You may be happy making only 10 percent on a quick sale, or you may need $75,000 a year to maintain your current lifestyle.

You may want to build net worth over time, seek continuous appreciation of your properties, and generate extra monthly income or enough rental cash flow to become financially independent.

You may want to buy a house and rent it out and patiently wait while your tenants pay off your mortgage. Maybe you love fixing up houses and want to buy a property, fix it up, and sell it. Or maybe you'd rather skip the work and just buy a house and sell it for immediate profit.

Maybe you're looking for a killing and are willing to lose your shirt if the chance to make a lot of money is involved. Or maybe, like me, you want to establish a full-time business that lets you achieve short-, medium-, and long-term goals.

Keeping a clear focus on your personal needs and goals will increase your likelihood of finding the right properties and minimize the risks to the downside of real estate investing. See Chapter 3 for a complete discussion of those risks.

Setting goals is one ingredient for business success. So is long-term commitment. I've never seen a get-rich-quick scheme that actually worked. And I've never met anybody who succeeded in an enterprise by working in it for just a year. If you don't make at least a three- to five-year commitment to your business, you most likely won't succeed.

It's the same story in real estate. To succeed, you need to make a long-term commitment, even if you're only planning to invest in real estate part-time. You also need a written plan, another crucial element of success. Can you imagine anyone accomplishing anything great without one? Thankfully, every time you fly in a plane, the pilot has a written plan and doesn't just start heading north and hope to get there!

Your written plan should specify your big goals and break each into short-, medium-, and long-term goals. For example, let's say your biggest goal is to be financially independent in seven years. If you determine that you need $5,000 each month to cover your expenses, and you know that every rental property will generate $250 each month in positive cash flow, you can calculate how many rental properties you will need. From there you can determine how many properties you will need to look at each week to find units worth buying, and how many properties you will need to purchase yearly to generate $60,000 each year seven years from now. Simple math will help you determine what you need to do this week, this month, six months from now, and by the end of the year to reach your goal.

Write your plan down! Revise your plan and your goals every six months. Include your loved ones in your goal setting. Be optimistic, but realistic. If you set a goal that is *too* high to reach, you'll be frustrated. Use the Formulating a Winning Strategy Worksheet at the end of this chapter to organize your thoughts and begin to make your plan. Start by writing down your goals in these areas:

- *Personal goals*—Do you want to spend more time with your family, take more vacations, buy a new boat?
- *Health goals*—Should you exercise more, quit smoking, lose weight?
- *Education goals*—What do you want to learn? Should you take courses in real estate, get another degree, read more books?
- *Spiritual goals*—Should you help people more, attend church or synagogue, improve yourself in some way?
- *Family goals*—What goals can you agree on together? Do you want to spend more time together, be more financially secure, get a better place to live?

- *Vacation and travel plans goals*—How much vacation time do you want, where do you want to go, and what do you want to do? (One of my goals was to take a one-month vacation each year. Now I take two months each year, and my next goal is to take a 100-day cruise around the world.)
- *Fun and hobbies goals*—How much leisure time do you want, and how will you spend it?
- *Career goals*—How far do you want to rise in your company? On your own? Do you want to quit your full-time job? What will you do instead?
- *Financial goals*—Which debts do you want to pay off? How much monthly income will you need? How much wealth do you want to accumulate in the next year?
- *Charitable goals*—How will you share your time and money? How will you help others? Which charities will you be involved with? Of all my activities, charity work is the most rewarding.

Take a Financial Snapshot

You need an accurate understanding of your current financial picture before you can offer a contract, apply for a loan, or seek a business partner. Later, you can look back on your financial snapshot to see how your circumstances have improved and how well you have met your financial goals.

Use the Financial Snapshot Worksheet at the end of this chapter to make an accurate summary of your current income, assets, and liabilities. Your snapshot will help determine how to get started in real estate investing. If you're broke, you obviously can't buy and hold and will need to use strategies that let you earn profits without investing any money of your own. On the other hand, if you have savings and investments, buying and holding is a real possibility.

Be sure to list all of your monthly expenses, including rent or mortgage, car payments, credit card bills, insurance, household expenses, tuition, and so forth.

Assess Your Personality

Understanding your personality type will help you recognize and succeed in finding a compatible corner of the real estate business.

If you love to work with your hands, maybe you should plan to buy and rehab one or two homes a year to make an extra $20,000 to $40,000.

If you enjoy solitude more than company, maybe you should focus on buying and flipping instead of buying and holding. If you still want to pursue landlording, maybe you should find a partner to manage the "people" aspects of your business.

No one can do everything. When you know what you're good at, you can concentrate in that area and leave the other responsibilities to someone else. For example, if you're a "big picture" person, you may need a detail-oriented partner. If you're strong on details, you may need a "big picture" partner.

Determine How Much Money and Time You Have to Invest

How many houses can you purchase? How much time can you spend on real estate? Use the Available Money and Time to Invest in Real Estate Worksheet at the end of this chapter to help answer these questions.

Be conservative in your estimates. It's important to understand that any time you borrow money, you must be sure you can pay it back, even if the economy slows or goes sour. Don't overestimate your time, either. Plenty of people tell me they want to get into real estate, but they're already working 70 hours a week and have a family. Perhaps they can manage six to eight hours a week to find a good deal and get something going. But the more time you can invest, the faster your business will grow and the stronger it will be.

Robert's Rules for Ethical Real Estate Investing

One of the reasons I went into real estate was to feel that I was making a difference in the world. I enjoyed my previous career working in securities, stocks, and bonds, and it was certainly lucrative. But at the end of the day, I would ask myself: How satisfying is this, really? What have I actually accomplished? Often it felt like all I was doing was helping people who already were making 13 percent interest on their money make 14 percent instead—in the end, a negligible accomplishment.

Through real estate, I *have* been able to make a difference. I've been a resource for many people with real estate problems they didn't know how to solve. I've turned ugly properties into attractive properties and created comfortable, affordable housing for families of limited means. My improvements have changed houses, blocks, neighborhoods, and communities as well as the lives of buyers, sellers, and renters. Through lease-optioning, I've helped homeless families become homeowners, affecting their families for generations to come. Owning a home lets parents build wealth and gives kids a more stable home life. Everybody is better off!

In my view, the best way to make money is by helping people. By doing the right thing, you can help people while also helping yourself to build a successful, happy, and ethical real estate investing career. I have helped people *and* made money by developing and following a number of principles in my business. First of all, everything I do has to meet three criteria:

1. It has to help someone.
2. It needs to be profitable.
3. It has to be fun.

If a deal doesn't meet these three criteria, I won't do it. I've passed up many potentially profitable transactions because I wouldn't have helped anyone. Of course, profit is basic to any business, so an unprofitable deal is out of the question.

Fun, yes. I get to meet some great people, I get to dress the way I like, and I never worry about impressing anyone. Oftentimes, I go downtown in shorts and a T-shirt, driving my plain car. Many of the bankers, lawyers, and professionals look at me like I am some kind of bum. I think it's funny. I don't have to wear a suit and tie to work or limit myself to two short weeks of vacation each year, yet I probably make more in three months than many of them make all year—and you can, too.

I strive to treat my customers (and that includes tenants) like they're valued, and make sure that everybody comes out a winner. (You'd be surprised how often people in real estate overlook these basic business principles. In fact, it's appalling.) And finally, I believe that everyone in business should use part of their business or time to help others. I try to use between 5 and 10 percent of my time and money to help others. Here are some other guidelines for an ethical real estate investing business:

- Strive to help people first, make money second. If you cannot help someone, a deal is probably not worth doing. I provide quality low- and moderate-income housing to help people and to make money. Many times, I have bought houses that were being foreclosed on. At foreclosure, the owners would get nothing. I often pay them tens of thousands of dollars, which helps them find a new home and saves their credit. I help them and I make a profit. For more ideas about helping others in real estate, visit my Web site at <www.shemin.com>.
- When you're just beginning in real estate, concentrate on donating some of your time or business to assisting others less fortunate. You could help the elderly repair their homes, counsel low-income families on budgeting and eventually buying a home, or volunteer to build a home with Habitat for Humanity. Later, you can make financial contributions as well. Find out about and take me up on my "Landlord Challenge," where I help homeless families become homeowners (see page 144 in Chapter 7).
- Never take advantage of people. Tell them what you're doing and how, and what the results are likely to be for all parties involved. Disclose what you are doing in writing.
- Never complete a real estate deal where everyone is not happy with the outcome.
- If you work with partners or investors, always pay them more than they expect. If you're in the business for the long term, you don't want a one-time killing; you want repeat business. Adding a cash bonus or percentage point or two to the return on a loan is a great way to ensure that the investor will want to do business with you again—and tell others about you.
- Treat renters with respect and provide them with quality housing.

No one gets ahead by harming other people—or if they do, their success doesn't last very long. Embrace the highest values and employ practices with the greatest integrity, and you are sure to take great pleasure in your efforts.

Formulating a Winning Strategy Worksheet

6 months	1 year	5 years	10 years	20 years

Personal goals:

Health goals:

Education goals:

Spiritual goals:

Family goals:

Vacation and travel plans goals:

Fun and hobbies goals:

Career goals:

Financial goals:

Charitable goals:

Financial Snapshot Worksheet

CURRENT JOB

Monthly income: Annual income:

Current savings: Current expenses:

Job satisfaction: (1–10):

CURRENT CREDIT: Excellent   Good   Fair   Bad

INVESTMENT SAVINGS
Home:
Car:
Furnishings:
Individual Retirement Account:

Life insurance:
Employee programs (401(k), pension):
Cash:
Stocks/bonds: Average yield:
Real estate:
Other:

Total assets:

DEBTS
Home loans:
Real estate loans:
Car loans:
Credit cards:
Other debt

Total debt:

Total assets:
Minus total debt:
Equals total net worth:

Available Money and Time to Invest in Real Estate Worksheet

(Remember to keep a cushion.)

Cash: Brokerage loans:

Credit lines: Private loans:

Equity line: Family loans:

Unencumbered assets: Credit cards (risky):

Individual Retirement Account:

Collateral to pledge for bank loans, including real estate, stocks, and bonds:

Banking relationships:

Income goals:

Cash flow for real estate wealth accumulation:

	Annual Income NEEDS	Annual Income GOALS	Actual Annual INCOME
Current			
1 year			
2 years			
3 years			
4 years			
5 years			
10 years			
15 years			
20 years			

Free hours or hours available to spend on real estate weekly:

1-5   6-10   11-20   21-30   31-40   41-50   51-60   61-70   71-80

CHAPTER 2

Ten Ways to Find
Profitable Properties

*Nothing in the world can take the place of persistence. Talent will not, nothing is
more common than unsuccessful men with talent. Genius will not, the world is full
of educated derelicts. Persistence and determination alone are omnipotent. The slo-
gan "press on" has solved and always will solve the problems of the human race.*

—Calvin Coolidge

 **ROBERT'S RULES**

You must always be searching for motivated sellers.
Remember, if a seller is not motivated, you will not find a good
deal.

Ever known someone who always seems to get a "deal" no matter
what they are buying? Just like cars, clothes, food, and stereos, there is
a "wholesale," or bargain market in real estate. That's where the good
deals are hidden.

All forms of making money as a real estate investor begin with finding a good deal: A motivated seller who will sell property at a discount of about 20 to 40 percent off its retail value. (Chapter 3 will discuss good deals in greater detail.) Whether you plan to buy and hold property, lease it, fix it up and sell it, or just be paid to find good deals for others (that is, be a "bird dog"), you must first find undervalued property. Without a good deal, you cannot make money in real estate. Finding and purchasing undervalued properties and turning them into instant or long-term profits is the key to making money and being successful in real estate.

Many people mistakenly think that to get a good deal in real estate you must take advantage of someone. This is absolutely not true. In a good real estate deal, you help someone who needs to sell a house or building and are able to contract for or purchase it for less than what it is worth—perhaps 60 to 80 cents on the dollar.

Why would someone sell a property for less than full value? Health problems, divorce, a death in the family, unemployment, balloon payments, estate sales, pending foreclosures, and landlord "burnout"—all are motivating factors for people to sell their real estate at a discount. Each situation may trigger a distress sale, in which the seller has to sell very quickly and must get as much cash as possible. Perhaps someone has died and left the house to an estate or to a widow, children, or relatives who no longer want to live in the house or cannot afford to make the payments. These survivors may want to get as much money as they can out of it, quickly and easily. Families in debt who cannot make mortgage payments may be facing foreclosure and eviction, a worse credit rating, and the costs of the foreclosure if the house is not sold quickly. All of these distress sales spell opportunities for you since your job as a real estate investor is to locate these people and help them.

This chapter discusses, in detail, ten ways to find undervalued or distressed properties. Some will strike you as simple, and they are. However, the simplest, most effective methods are often the most overlooked, even by so-called experts, and you don't need to master or practice all ten. I know everyday real estate investors who make a living just by utilizing one or two of the following methods:

1. Local newspapers
2. Driving for dollars
3. Foreclosures
4. Auctions

5. Tax sales
6. "Bird dogs"
7. Advertising
8. Real estate agents
9. Real estate investment associations
10. Networking

Let's examine them one at a time.

Local Newspapers

Newspapers are a cheap and easy way to find good deals and educate yourself about the market in which you will be investing. By reading the newspaper regularly, you quickly will learn what markets, house types, and prices make the most sense for you. The newspaper lists properties by areas, certain features, and also sometimes by price. By analyzing newspaper ads and getting in your car and looking at some of the real estate, you'll discover what "retail value" means, what "good values" are, and where to find the bargains.

Saturday and Sunday editions of the newspaper are the best. Look through the whole section, but specifically for properties listed under *Investments* in areas in which you plan to concentrate, particularly noting For Sale by Owners (FSBOs). I also like to look at For Rent ads, because they can lead me to motivated landlords or owners who may be willing to sell at a discount. (Chapter 3 will discuss how to decide where to concentrate.) You'll also be alerted to upcoming real estate auctions. Be sure to check out all local papers, neighborhood weeklies, and any other newspaper that has real estate ads.

NEWSPAPERS

Advantages: Easy to do. No real cost to you.

Disadvantages: Everyone has access to the newspaper, so competition is fierce.

Many people make a living just from the newspaper. In fact, that's where I've found some of my best deals. Be aware, though, competition is fierce. When I find a good deal in the newspaper, I call immediately, because I know that if the deal is really that good, someone else may beat me to it.

Driving for Dollars

I know a young man who spends every Saturday driving up and down streets looking for vacant houses and people who need to sell their houses in a hurry for below-market prices. He copies down the addresses of vacant houses, records phone numbers listed on For Sale signs, and talks to neighbors and strangers. He finds great deals, puts them under contract, and sells them to other investors for some big dollars. He makes thousands of dollars per house and never seems to be lacking inventory—simply by driving through neighborhoods!

Driving through neighborhoods is a highly effective way to locate undervalued properties. I do it myself. Recently, by spending an hour and a half in the car, I found six potentially great deals that I eventually made thousands of dollars of profit on.

When you drive around a neighborhood, compile a list of phone numbers and addresses for the properties that interest you and then follow up on them. "FSBO" properties are for sale without the aid of a real estate agent, so you can negotiate directly with the seller, who may be in a hurry to sell the property.

For Rent properties probably are owned by a real estate investor and/or managed by a property management company. If the unit is empty and not generating any income, the owner may be motivated to sell the property. Contact the owner or the property management company directly, and let it be known that you are interested in purchasing the property. The property management company also may be a good source for finding other owners who are motivated to sell their properties.

Regular real estate company For Sale signs also are worth following up on. You will get a good idea of what retail value is when you compare other homes in the neighborhood, and you actually may find a good deal.

Look for abandoned properties, vacant or boarded-up houses, houses in need of serious repair, and houses with unkempt or trash-filled yards. Houses with "Condemned" or "Uninhabitable" signs can also be

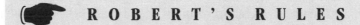

ROBERT'S RULES

A small, unprofessional-looking, or difficult-to-spot For Sale or For Rent sign could mean a better deal for you. Because the sellers are not marketing their property effectively, you may be the only one who realizes that the property is even for sale.

gold mines. In almost every case, the owner of such a property either has to, or would very much like to, get rid of it. Houses may be condemned and deemed unfit for human habitation for many reasons, including health and safety factors (they may have had fires, their plumbing or electrical systems may not be safe, etc.). Some condemned houses need a lot of work, while others may have a simple, easy-to-fix plumbing, electrical, or roof problem. Many serious real estate professionals who buy properties in bad shape, fix them up, and sell them at a profit deal only in condemned properties and make a great living. Contact your local Code Administrator (at the local City Housing Offices) for a list of code violations and/or reasons why the house has been condemned.

Get the addresses of any and all vacant properties, and those that need major and minor repairs, and find out who the owners are and how you can contact them. One of the most successful tactics that I have used is talking to neighbors. (You'll find them outside if you survey a neighborhood on a Saturday or Sunday, or in the evening.) Neighbors can provide a wealth of information. They may be able to tell you who the owners are, where they are, and why the property is abandoned or in disrepair. The neighbors also may be able to tell you about other properties that fit your criteria.

If you have a lot of addresses, you may want to call or visit the tax assessor's office, where the ownership of all houses is on public record, or the Registrar of Deeds' office. The employees there should be helpful. Many city and state tax rolls are in a database that can be accessed online on the Internet so you can look up the owners. Also, most real estate agents will be glad to help you in hopes that they can make you a client.

Follow up with a phone call or letter to the owners indicating that you may be interested in buying their property.

Driving through neighborhoods is an inexpensive, easy way to learn more about them. You'll learn what the neighbors and neighborhood are like, get an idea of prices and rents in that area, and perhaps, most importantly, get an idea of which neighborhoods are "in transition"—where the houses are being fixed up and property values seem to be on the rise. If you can find a deal in one of those neighborhoods, don't hesitate to buy it. If you find neighborhoods in disrepair that are sinking down and getting worse, stay away!

DRIVING FOR DOLLARS

Advantages: You will find many good deals. There is simply no better way to learn about a neighborhood.

Disadvantages: Takes time and patience. Be careful when getting out and looking at houses. If you are in a tough neighborhood, take someone with you.

Foreclosures

A foreclosure occurs when property owners have not paid their mortgage and the lending institution, such as a bank, the Federal Housing Administration (FHA), or the Department of Veterans Affairs (VA), has taken or is in the process of taking back the property due to non-payment. The foreclosure process, which can take from 30 days to a year depending on the state, takes place through an attorney, title company, or the court system.

The top reasons why houses are foreclosed on include missed payments due to job interruption, health problems, and divorce. It often takes two incomes to support a family and make the house payments and divorce usually takes away one income, making the house unaffordable. Unemployment or the death of the breadwinner also can cause a house to go into foreclosure. So can unexpected bills or expenses that change the property owner's financial position, especially ongoing medical procedures or problems that must be paid for out of pocket.

R O B E R T ' S   R U L E S

Safety is a concern when you visit transitional neighborhoods. It's best to err on the side of caution. Good safety precautions include the following:

- Always get permission to enter a house from the owner.

- Never go into a dangerous area or get out of your car if you do not feel safe.

- Always be aware of who is around you. If someone is nearby who makes you uncomfortable, leave immediately.

- Do not drive expensive or flashy cars into transitional or low-income neighborhoods.

Failure to meet a mortgage balloon payment—a 10- to 20-year mortgage in which the balance is due in 3 to 10 years—can trigger a foreclosure. And sometimes people move out of town or are transferred in their job and just let the house go. If they have too much debt, they simply walk away from their house and let it be foreclosed on.

The VA guarantees home loans for veterans so that they can buy houses, but when veterans do not make their mortgage payments, the VA has to take back their house. The Department of Housing and Urban Development (HUD) and/or the FHA help first-time homebuyers buy a house by guaranteeing the loans. When first-time homebuyers get in over their head or come into financial trouble and cannot make their mortgage payments, HUD and the FHA also may reclaim these houses and offer them for sale. Both HUD and the VA list their foreclosure properties in the newspaper. You also can get a list of properties from your local HUD and/or VA office or through a real estate agent. To find out about the various lists of foreclosures, visit my Web site at <www.shemin.com>.

HUD and the VA constantly are taking back houses and offering them at below-market prices with attractive financing. You will have to shop hard and search intensely to find bargains that meet your own criteria, but they do exist. For the first year and a half that I was in real estate, I bought almost exclusively from the HUD list. HUD was offering very attractive financing on duplexes with 15 percent down. These financing packages are available around the country, though they may differ by region.

Banks, finance companies, shopping mall loan companies, and second mortgage companies also have to take back real estate. When one of these institutions repossesses a property, it is known as a bank repossession, or "repo." Most banks and lending institutions do not want to be in the real estate business and are very anxious to sell this real estate and get it "off the books." That means opportunity for the savvy real estate investor who can negotiate. If a bank has a $50,000 mortgage on a house with a market value of $80,000, the bank often will forego trying to make a profit so long as it can recover the initial loan plus costs. It may be possible to buy that house for $20,000 to $30,000 below the market value of the property. The extent of the opportunity depends on your local economy and the state of health of the lending institutions. For example, while some banks take a lot of properties back and look to sell them as quickly as possible, others do not take many properties back and are not as anxious to sell them. Nevertheless, there are always properties being foreclosed.

 R O B E R T ' S   R U L E S

Develop good relationships with your local banks and lending institutions, and you may be the first person they call when they want to get rid of a property quickly.

To foreclose, a lending institution must publish a notice that it is going to foreclose on a property. Many cities, municipalities, counties, and various areas of the country have a legal newspaper in which these public notices appear. Ask a knowledgeable attorney or bank officer where foreclosures are publicized and subscribe to this publication. A bank's Real Estate Owned ("REO") Department or Special Asset Department also can provide a list of repossessed properties and their corresponding prices. Even though these notices use very legal language and may appear difficult to read, this list is an incredible source of real estate that you can buy for below-market values. It is imperative that you find out where foreclosures are publicized and learn to use those lists.

Probably one of the best sources of undervalued properties can be found in the foreclosures of the second-tier lending institutions. The Money Store, Associates Financial, American General, Beneficial, and similar institutions lend to people who have been turned down by the banks. Because some of their customers do not have great credit, they only loan about 65 to 80 percent of the house value. When a loan goes bad and a borrower fails to make payments, the finance company may foreclose or just have the borrowers sign over the loan to them. Like banks, these companies are not in the real estate business and may be willing to sell a house for the outstanding loan.

Find these institutions and cultivate a friendship with their managers. Look in your yellow pages under Finance Companies. Ask to speak with the manager and let him or her know what you do. Inquire if they have any property for sale, and ask them to call you or send you a list of new foreclosures on a continuing basis. I recommend calling 10 to 20 finance companies each month to see what properties are available. Many of these institutions will offer you financing as well.

Deed of Trust or Mortgage State?

Before you begin to pursue foreclosure properties, find out whether your state is a *deed of trust* state or a *mortgage* state. (A real estate agent, a title company, or another investor can tell you.) When a loan is placed on a property in a deed of trust state, the property title is held in the name of a third party or trustee. If the note or mortgage is not paid, then the trustee is instructed to foreclose or take back the property. Because no court action is needed, foreclosures in deed of trust states may be complete in 30 to 90 days. In a mortgage state, no trustee is appointed. When a mortgage goes unpaid, whoever made the mortgage or loan must petition the court to foreclose—a much lengthier process. In both deed of trust and mortgage states, public notice of the foreclosure must be given (generally in a legal newspaper) before the action, but the time will vary by state.

Public Records Can Be Your Gold Mine

One of the most successful real estate wheeler-dealers in my town gets more leads than he ever needs about foreclosures and distress sales of real estate because he has befriended people in the courthouse and the Registrar of Deeds. He visits them almost every day, and even brings them treats. Needless to say, they are happy to direct him to newly recorded documents concerning foreclosures.

Public records can alert you to foreclosures or property that will soon be in foreclosure. Depending on your state, you may be able to find Sheriff's or Commissioner's notices of sale, or foreclosure notices. In trustee states, be on the lookout for notices of trustees' sales or notices of defaults. A simple review of the court docket also may reveal foreclosure judgments.

Each locality may call these things by different names, but your local courthouse officials, Registrar of Deeds, or an attorney easily can explain all of this to you. Find out from your local courthouse where notices of foreclosures are filed and which courts handle foreclosures and proceedings against homeowners or mortgagors (the people who borrowed money and are in debt). Ask your local Registrar of Deeds or any title insurance company about the foreclosure procedure in your area, and which publication they advertise in. (A sample notice of foreclosure is included in Appendix C.)

Many property records also are available on the Internet. Visit my Web site <www.shemin.com> to get references to foreclosure listings nationwide or call your local Registrar of Deeds for a list of online services in your area.

When you visit the courthouse, learn how the foreclosure system works and how to look up and gather information on properties. At first, the records may seem overwhelming, but with a little persistence and a lot of questions, you easily will be able to understand them. To succeed in investing in distressed properties, you need to know how your public records system works. Employees are paid to help answer your questions, so they'll be more than happy to explain.

You can find most real estate records in a general index kept on microfiche cards or computerized printouts. Once you find the name of a person who is in default or who is a mortgagor or owner of a property, look up that name in the general index. Almost all documents pertaining to that person or that property are filed there. Many localities use a filing system, called the book and page system, in which property information is recorded in a particular book and on a particular page, which you can find in the general index. Once you find what you are looking for by name, the index will refer you to the book and page where the information is recorded. Major metropolitan areas have a reel and image system, which is a microfiche or a computer system on which you may view the documents.

After you master the ins and outs of the system, you can look at many properties very rapidly. Once you find the information you need, the document numbers and the date should be easy to locate.

By going to the courthouse and reviewing documents, you'll soon learn how to look up and understand mortgages, judgments, taxes, abstracts of title, liens, IRS and state tax liens, *lis pendens,* trust deeds, and all other types of liens and real estate documents. Before you buy *any* property, but especially before you purchase a distressed property or a property in foreclosure, research every deed, trust, or lien recorded against that property. Some of these claims may make it impossible for you to take title to the property. Be sure to check the significance of your findings with an attorney.

FORECLOSURES

Advantages: Opportunities for great deals. You also can get some good financing from the foreclosing institution such as the bank, HUD, or the VA.

Disadvantages: Be careful. Just because something is in foreclosure does not mean it is a good deal. Why was it foreclosed on? Research liens and judgments carefully to avoid title problems. Get title insurance.

Auctions

Auctions are another source of properties priced below market value and although I have found some really good deals at auctions, to be honest, they are few and far between.

Auctions are gaining in popularity because they offer a quick, easy, and exciting way to sell a house. Listing the house with a real estate agent or going the FSBO route can mean waiting months until the "right" buyer comes along. Selling in a hurry may be preferable even if the seller thinks an agent can get a higher price. However, as auctions become more common, many auction houses are now selling close to or even above full value.

AUCTIONS

Advantages: Auctions are quick, fun, and educational. You will learn market values from the auction price and meet other real estate people from whom you can buy and sell. If you go to enough of them, you eventually may get an incredible deal.

Disadvantages: With all of the excitement at auctions, many properties sell for right at or above true value. Do not get emotional. Stay calm and directed.

Attending auctions will give you a first-class education in real estate. An auction represents the highest form of capitalism. You will see demand, supply, and various market forces in action. The price at which a house sells at auction is typically an accurate indication of market value, because the heavily publicized auction draws people interested in purchasing that type of property.

Even more important, you will meet many other people who are interested in or are buying investment real estate. At every auction I work the crowd as though it is the most important cocktail party of my life. I try to meet everyone, get their names and phone numbers, and find out what they do. I know that later they will become customers for my properties.

Look for auctions in the newspaper or call local auction companies and ask to be notified of each and every auction. Cultivate auctioneers. Ask them about other auctions and other property. They are excellent sources of good deals and sometimes will sell a property to you before an auction has been publicized.

Auctions can be educational, profitable, and a whole lot of fun. In the end, the most valuable information you'll get from an auction are names for your network list of people who buy and sell properties.

 R O B E R T ' S   R U L E S

Secrets of Bidding at an Auction

1. Inspect the house and the information very carefully. Ask the following questions, as the answers will help you in your bidding:
   a. Will title insurance be provided?
   b. How long do I have to close the purchase?
   c. Is the purchase cash or terms?
   d. Are there any public notices of problems, for example, code letters? Can I test the appliances, heating, and air?
   e. How much earnest money do I have to put down?
   f. What repairs are needed and how much will they cost?

2. Based on this information, set your highest bid before the bidding begins.

3. Never bid until the final count. Only the last bidder wins at an auction, and the truly serious bidders come out at the end. I never bid until the down count begins —after the auctioneer says "going twice. . . ."

4. Test your opponent's patience. If you get into a bidding contest, raise your bid by only $25 to $75 to annoy your opponent. This takes the excitement and emotion out of the bidding and the other bidder may give up.

5. Never get caught up in the emotion of the auction and never bid above your highest bid. Remember, real estate is a business. Let logic, not emotion, rule your decisions.

Estate Sales

Estate sales are another excellent source of undervalued properties. Simply stay in regular contact with attorneys who specialize in estate planning—get a list from the Bar Association. When family needs and conflicts necessitate a quick sale of an estate, you'll hear about it. It's also a good idea to stay in touch with the probate agency in your city to determine the estate executor on file. Some people send letters and make phone calls to the obituary list in the newspaper to see if the family has a house that it may want to sell. This may sound morbid, but you actually can help out a family that wants to sell quickly and isn't sure how.

ESTATE SALES

Advantages: Sellers may be extremely motivated.

Disadvantages: Clearing the title may be time consuming and complicated if several children or grandchildren inherited the property. Your attorney or title company will need to track down all heirs before title can pass to you.

Tax Sales

The IRS, state, and local taxing authorities all have the power and the ability to slap a powerful tax lien on a property when the owners don't pay their taxes. If the tax lien is not removed by paying the relevant taxing authority, these agencies seize the property and sell it at a tax sale.

Each area of the country does a tax sale a little differently, but basically they are like auctions given by some of the most powerful auctioneers in the country: the IRS or the local and state taxing authorities. The process begins when an individual does not pay taxes, allowing a taxing authority to place a tax lien on the property. This tax lien takes precedence over all other liens, mortgages, and debt. After a period of time, the taxing authorities will auction off property to collect on the tax lien. Even after an investor has purchased the property, the owner usually can exercise a "right of redemption" and reclaim the property by paying back taxes. In that case, the investor is refunded his or her money plus 10 to 20 percent interest on the sum. Tax auctions are publicized in the local newspaper, but you also can find out about them by calling the IRS and/or the state and local taxing authorities.

TAX SALES

Advantages: A good return on your money can be realized, even if the original owners redeem their property, and sometimes you literally can "steal" a property.

Disadvantages: You give up the property if the original owner seeks a right of redemption. Also, in many areas it is difficult to get title insurance on a property purchased at a tax sale. Find out from a local attorney, the tax office, or a title company if you can get title insurance.

Bird Dogs

Many real estate professionals have a network of people who find undervalued properties for them. These "bird dogs" sniff out and point toward a property that may turn out to be a very good deal. A bird dog can be anyone who can say, "Hey, here's a house, an address, and/or the name of an owner who may want to sell this property at a greatly reduced price" or "I saw a boarded-up house at 20 Main Street." Friends, acquaintances, mortgage company employees, attorneys, accountants, real estate agents, other real estate investors, government employees, public works employees, maintenance people, property managers, and landscapers all make excellent bird dogs.

Let everyone know that you are in the business of buying real estate and it will be amazing how many people will help you—especially if you pay them. If someone brings you an address, the name of an owner, or someone who needs to sell a property at a reduced price, and you buy that property and later turn it into profits for yourself, pay the person a finder's fee. This will ensure that your bird dog will continue to look for properties and good deals for you.

I use bird dogs often. I offer $500 cash if I close (that is, purchase) a property that someone has found for me. Of course, the amount you pay your bird dogs may vary depending on how much you can make on a deal. Make sure that you and your bird dog understand that the fee is not due until you close on the property. Do not pay for leads that may not turn into anything.

 R O B E R T ' S   R U L E S

Have your bird dogs bring you names, phone numbers, and addresses of boarded-up houses and other potential deals, notices of estate sales, names of anybody getting divorced, or anyone who needs to sell a house quickly. If you get an address, great! Just call the tax assessor's office to find the owner, have a real estate agent look it up, or find it on the Internet.

Warning: Many states prohibit real estate agents from paying finder's fees. If you are a real estate agent, check with your broker or company to find out if using bird dogs or paying finder's fees is allowed.

BIRD DOGS

Advantages: Bird dogs free up your personal time because others are doing your legwork and finding you great deals.

Disadvantages: Bird dogs cost money. You must pay your bird dogs so they keep calling you and not someone else. Like any business, it's hard to find people who will work so it may take a while to find good bird dogs.

Advertising

Promote Yourself

One way to find undervalued properties is to advertise yourself as someone who buys properties. Look in your newspaper and find ads that say "Cash for your house" or "Need to sell your house, please call this number." Run ads like these in your local and neighborhood newspapers and "shoppers," and people who need to sell their homes quickly will call you.

Here are several extremely effective ads, written by one of the top copywriters in the nation. Try them and you'll see why they were well worth the top fees he charges.

DO YOU NEED A MONEY MIRACLE RIGHT NOW? If you have a house in any condition that you want to sell, I've got cash, know-how, and banking connections, and I'm eager to buy your house. Please call Joe Buyer at 000-0000 right now for an extraordinary, no-risk proposition.

ARE YOU STARVED FOR CASH? Do you have a house you want to sell? I've got cash, know-how, and banking connections and I'm itching to buy your house. I urge you to call Jane Buyer at 000-0000 right now for an extraordinary, no-risk proposition.

ARE YOU BEHIND IN YOUR HOUSE PAYMENTS? Do you want to sell your house? I've got cash, know-how, and banking connections and I'm itching to buy your house. I urge you to call Joe Buyer at 000-0000 right now for an extraordinary, no-risk proposition.

WARNING! SELL NO HOUSE UNTIL YOU READ THIS: Do you want to sell your house? I've got cash, know-how, and banking connections and I'm itching to buy your house. I urge you to call Jane Buyer at 000-000 right now for an extraordinary, no-risk proposition.

Top Real Estate Owner Looking for Six Houses to Pay Cash for This Week! Have you got a house you want to sell? I've got cash, know-how, and banking connections and I'm itching to buy your house. I urge you to call Joe Buyer at 000-000 right now for an extraordinary, no-risk proposition.

A friend of mine once bought very cheaply an abandoned building next to a busy highway for the sole purpose of painting "I Buy Real Estate" and his phone number on the side facing the highway. This free billboard, his sole form of advertising, is viewed by over 10,000 people every day and has helped him successfully find undervalued properties for more than 12 years.

Business cards also are another effective way to advertise yourself. Print up business cards that say, "I buy houses," or "I'll pay cash for your house." Give them to everyone you meet. Distribute as many cards as possible.

Use Direct Mail to Spread the Word

Direct mail advertising also can bring you new leads. Many real estate professionals will get lists of names of motivated sellers from the county courthouse, the phone book, or other marketing sources and send out multitudes of letters introducing themselves and letting the world know that they buy houses for cash. Those motivated sellers include:

- Long-time owners whose mortgages may have been paid down or off
- Owners of multiple properties (they may be disgruntled landlords or just feel they own too much)
- Out-of-town or out-of-state owners
- Owners of boarded-up or condemned houses
- Owners in "transition" areas

Letters can let people know what business you're in and bring you many potentially good properties. The following ideas will help make your direct mail advertising more effective:

- Never send a letter bulk mail. It looks too much like junk mail and may get thrown out before it's read.
- Use a first-class commemorative stamp on your letter to increase the odds that the recipient opens the envelope.
- Never use an adhesive address label on the envelope.
- Never place any sort of teaser copy on the envelope. It is a good idea to write "Urgent" in red on the outer envelope.

- Place your address only in the upper left-hand corner of the envelope.
- Make sure the recipient's name and address and your return address are in the same typeface and look as if they were typed by the same typewriter, in order to make the correspondence appear as personal as possible. A laser printer can do an excellent job.
- Always test a mailing list first by sending out no more than 1,000 letters at any one time. Make sure the results warrant mailing to the entire list.
- Let people in on the reason why you are making them an offer and you'll increase your response considerably.
- Make the right offer to the right list. For example, tell out-of-state owners that you can help them stop worrying about their property and take away the headaches it may be causing.
- Offer cash and a quick close. Most people will not accept any other terms at first. Hook them with cash and negotiate later!
- Ask for a specific action, for example, "Please call me at 000-0000 before such-and-such a date."
- Make it easy to respond. Include your telephone numbers and street and e-mail addresses so prospects can choose how to contact you. Include an 800 number in letters to out-of-state owners.
- Ask for referrals. Include a return card that asks, "Do you know anyone else who wants to sell?" Include space for names and numbers.

Compiled lists that you rent or buy for your direct mail literature let you broadcast your message to a wide audience, but mailing to a list of contacts that you have gathered yourself generally will out-pull a rented "cold" mailing list by a factor of 25:1.

Pass Out and Post Flyers

Passing out and posting flyers also can help you find undervalued properties. Place them in mailboxes in the neighborhoods you target, and you should get some good responses. Give flyers to real estate agents, property managers, and anyone else who may be a potential "bird dog."

Put them on bulletin boards at grocery stores, churches, and community centers. Here's an example of a particularly effective sign/flyer:

DO YOU WANT IMMEDIATE CASH FOR YOUR HOME?
HOME CAN BE IN ANY AREA & IN ANY CONDITION!
CALL JOE BUYER RIGHT NOW!!
000-0000.
We guarantee results quickly and safely.
We can close in 24 hours if needed.

Offer a Free Educational Seminar

You should consider holding an educational seminar at a well-located public library. In your ads and direct mail piece, offer to educate your prospect for free by discussing such topics as "What to Do to Get More Money If You're Thinking of Selling Your House," or "Can You Make More Money Selling Your House Yourself?" or "How to Get Top Equity Out of Your House!" You also can bring in different speakers (bankers, mortgage firms, etc.) willing to talk about subjects of interest (e.g., loans, refinancing, how to buy more property by trading your existing house, saving money on points, joint venture investing, free evaluation). You can tell attendees, "If you qualify, we can buy your house in one day flat and we will turnkey the entire project for you."

Experiment with each of these advertising methods to see which works best for you! The most cost-efficient way to advertise may not be the cheapest.

ADVERTISING

Advantages: Keeps your name and number out among the public, and you *will* find some good deals.

Disadvantages: Can be expensive and response can be hit-or-miss. Sometimes people call you, sometimes they don't.

Real Estate Agents

Real estate agents can be an excellent source of locating undervalued properties and determining their market value, especially for beginning investors. Down the road, they also can be a great resource for selling the properties.

Many real estate agents have access to computers and books called the Multiple Listing Service (MLS), which is a directory of all houses listed for sale through agents. Using these resources, agents can narrow a search and find the types of properties that you are looking for (e.g., nonqualifying loans, fixer-uppers, etc.). They also can help you determine the true value of these properties by using comparable sales of other properties in the neighborhood.

REAL ESTATE AGENTS

Advantages: Real estate agents are excellent sources of good deals and good market information. Many specialize in working with investors and can find nonqualifying or owner's terms properties.

Disadvantages: Agent commissions are based on the sales price, thus increasing your costs. Make sure you know who the agent represents. Most of the time, the agent represents the seller. You may want to think about becoming an agent yourself to get part of the commission.

Let real estate agents work for you as bird dogs. Tell every agent in your area that you are looking for undervalued properties, and the price range you desire. Because they make a commission off every house they sell, they're always looking for buyers. Although most of the deals they present will not meet your criteria, thank them for calling and encourage them to call again. Eventually, one of these agents will present you with the right deal.

I've used real estate agents since I started my business, and I still use them. Because my job is to find good deals and move them quickly, I would rather pay an agent a commission to drive potential buyers around to properties, handle paperwork, and so forth. I can use my time finding new deals.

Real Estate Investment Associations

A real estate investment club is a group of investors that gets together every few weeks to trade investment ideas. They let each other know what properties they have for sale, what they're looking for, and exchange tips on how to find properties or how to be a better landlord. These clubs are excellent places to meet other people in real estate and find properties that may be very good deals. You'll also gain knowledge and enjoy camaraderie, and when you have a piece of property to sell, other members will be your first buyers. You can visit my Web site at <www.shemin.com> to find the real estate investment association in your area, which you should join. If an association does not already exist, perhaps you can start one.

REAL ESTATE INVESTMENT ASSOCIATIONS

Advantages: These are great ways to meet other investors, contractors, buyers, and sellers. You can learn a lot of good information and find a mentor.

Disadvantages: None.

Network

A strong network is a key ingredient in succeeding in real estate. As an investor, you are looking for motivated sellers and buyers. You want to find good deals, and you want to identify prospective buyers who are looking for good deals. To build a network of people who can help you and ensure that you profit in the long run, meet as many people as you can and keep a list of their names, addresses, phone numbers, and related information.

Get out on the street and knock on doors. Call on banks, savings and loans, finance firms, and credit unions to determine if they own particular properties they may want to sell. Visit builders who have either gone "belly up" or are under financial pressure to sell (it is also possible that some builders have incomplete houses or trade-ins they want to salvage). Approach attorneys, accountants, and financial planners to determine if they have clients in need.

Because foreclosures, estate sales, and divorces can be good sources of great real estate deals, you should contact as many attorneys as possible and let them know that you buy real estate. Identify and set up meetings with the big foreclosure attorneys in your area. Constantly remind them that you buy. They also may be able to put you in contact with lending institutions that are foreclosing on property.

It is possible that these attorneys and lending institutions already let their friends or other investors know about the "good deals." Make yourself one of these people. Take the attorneys out to lunch and send them thank-you letters. Be advised, however, of the attorney ethics rules. Some attorneys may not be able to tell you anything, depending on the circumstances, because they have to protect their clients' identities.

Accountants or CPAs are another good source of real estate deals. They may know of other investors or of divorces, estate sales, and other special situations in which people in financial trouble need to sell. Contractors also should be part of your network, because they are often the first to hear about distressed properties.

When you approach other professionals, why not ask them to serve as an informal board of advisors? Accountants, bankers, attorneys, contractors, and other investors also can help by reviewing packages and looking at business plans. Get their opinions before you seek financing for a deal.

Try to make these relationships reciprocal. When my contractors, bankers, and attorneys bring me deals, I try to return the favor by bringing them more clients and business.

Most of my best deals have come from other real estate investors who are also out there uncovering good deals. Sometimes these investors lack the necessary funds to buy a really solid deal. To make sure

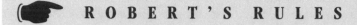

ROBERT'S RULES

Serious real estate investors need access to a good real estate attorney and CPA. Shop around and find someone who is active in real estate. Not only will that person be an excellent and much-needed advisor to your business, but probably a source of deals as well.

they don't miss a profit opportunity, they will call me to take advantage of the deal and take a commission or finder's fee.

Get names, addresses, and phone numbers every time you meet a real estate agent, see an ad in the newspaper, have someone respond to an ad, bump into a likely prospect at an auction, meet real estate club members, visit accountants or attorneys who specialize in real estate, or learn of a group of homebuyers. Someone on your list might be thinking of moving. Or perhaps you've sold that person a property before and have thereby gained trust. Or maybe a prospect can put you in touch with a friend or relative who's interested in buying a property. Maybe someone wants to sell an existing house quickly as part of a divorce settlement. Maybe a relative died and the estate wants to unload some properties quickly. Maybe a prospect has reached an age when he or she wants to be a passive investor. All of these situations can benefit you.

I've heard every excuse for not starting the compilation process. I've concluded that the single biggest enemy is inertia. No one can get you to succeed in spite of yourself. But the rewards are worth it. Compile a list, and you can compete with the best real estate professional on the planet and end up the winner.

Don't delay! Start gathering your list of prospective buyers and sellers now! Believe me, your career in real estate depends on your prospect list. With a good list, you can take virtually any real estate business and, by regularly mailing offers and information and telemarketing to your list, double or triple your profits in a matter of six months.

Use Letters and Phone Calls to Locate Sellers and Buyers

Personalized letters to individuals in your network can generate terrific response. Personalize the following letter to the recipient and attach a dollar bill to the top of the letter. (From time to time I will attach a bright shiny penny instead.)

Dear _____ :

As you can see, I have attached a brand new dollar to the top of this letter. Why have I done this? There are two reasons:

1. I have something extremely important to tell you and I needed some way to be absolutely certain this letter catches your attention.

2. Because what I am writing about can make you a great deal of money, I thought using a dollar bill as a financial eye-catcher was quite appropriate.

Here's what it's all about:

Complete the letter by revealing the benefits of doing business with you. Here are some examples:

- I understand that you have a for sale by owner piece of property that you are attempting to sell.
- I understand that you have a distressed piece of property you are trying to sell.
- I understand that you have invested in distressed property in the past. I have two excellent duplexes that I believe are tremendous investments. I also believe I can structure a venture that will net you, at the very least, $10,000, but more likely $15,000 to $25,000 in bottom-line profits. Plus, I'm willing to take the bulk of the risk.

Sincerely,

Your Name

Three days after mailing this letter, telephone the prospect and say, "Hello, Mr. Jones? This is Jane Seller. Did you receive a letter recently with a dollar bill attached to it? You did? Good. I just wanted to check and see if you received it. You can't always trust the mail service these days. Isn't that right?"

(Note: That's two "yes" responses you've received!) "I just want to ask you if the dollar bill was still attached when you received it? It was? Great."

(Note: That's the third "yes"!) At this point you can merely ask if he or she would like to set up a date and time to discuss your proposal.

You can address a similar letter to a real estate attorney. Again, it should be personalized.

Dear _____ :

My name is _____ , and I have a proposition for you that quite possibly can bring you more clients. Fact is, if you've been looking for an effective and yet low-key way to market your services and improve the visibility of your practice, perhaps I can be of assistance.

I specialize in locating and rehabilitating distressed property. My service in the community is a well-accepted fact, because I have a successful track record in the low- and middle-income area that few real estate people get involved with.

I'm looking to have a longstanding relationship with an attorney who comes into contact with the types of properties that I am seeking. If you are that attorney, I would like to set up an appointment with you at your convenience.

I will have my secretary call you in the next few days to set up a meeting. For both of our benefits, I hope you will avail yourself of this splendid opportunity.

Sincerely,

Your Name

This letter can be used to tap into an investment professional's client base.

Dear _____ :

You probably have clients who are seeking safe, secure real estate investments. And perhaps it would be to their benefit if you were to point out these unique investments. I'm talking about investments that take the guesswork out of real estate property ownership.

If you would like, I would be happy to have lunch or a cup of coffee with you to share some rather unique ideas. I would be happy to show you a number of properties that I believe are exceptional values. I would do this solely as a service to you and your clients.

Obviously, tapping into my client base could be a way to improve the marketing of your professional services, which I also will be happy to discuss with you.

For my part, I am looking for a long and enduring relationship—one based on your and your clients' needs. I will not simply show you the kinds of properties that would be in my self-interest to sell.

I think you'll find that I am quite knowledgeable in the field and do uncover exceptional values. And when I discover an uncommon value, I'll merely ask you if it is something a client of yours may be interested in.

I can't be any fairer than that. Because we both have a complex schedule, I will call you in a few days and see if we can find an available free moment to get together.

Sincerely,

Your Name

P.S. Our meeting may change your entire thinking about real estate investments and how to identify and bring in new clients. And it may change your clients' ideas on how to obtain alternate financing for specific projects. My business has grown rapidly because of this type of information, and I would appreciate the time to share it with you.

 R O B E R T ' S   R U L E S

Develop an active, ongoing action marketing plan that includes advertising, direct mail, telemarketing, seminars, and counseling services. Experiment with different ads, letters, and telemarketing strategies. What you're looking for is not how many prospects respond, but how many properties you actually close on. If you spend $60 every week on mailings to 100 people and you get a 2 percent response, you will generate 20 new prospects every ten-week period.

CHAPTER 3

Analyzing Properties

As a general rule, the most successful person in life is the one who has the best information.

—Benjamin Disraeli

Okay. The word is out. You're in real estate. You're looking at properties. You're learning. You're talking to real estate agents. You're talking to banks. You're looking at the Housing and Urban Development (HUD) list. You're running ads. You're responding to ads. You're beginning to cut through the theory and mystery and seeing how you can create a winning business.

If you're like I was at this stage, however, you have absolutely no past experience in real estate, so you're more than a little uptight. You're wondering not only if you're going to survive, but whether you'll have a chance to flourish.

To look to the future with confidence and profit accordingly, you need to take the guesswork out of real estate investments. This means arming yourself with the best possible information about the seller, the property, the neighborhood, the market, and potential buyers. And it means buying a property right, because the last thing you want is to be constantly weathering cash flow storms or "hidden" disasters that leech away your profit.

The key to surviving and flourishing is to have a clear grasp of the goals you established in Chapter 1, and to analyze every property *before you make an offer* to make sure that it is the kind of "good deal" that will help you meet your goals.

Doing this kind of thorough investigation or "due diligence" on every property will lessen the risks inherent in real estate investing. Be aware, though, no investment is risk free. A real estate investment, like any other, can go sour. In my experience, the following factors can put a real estate enterprise at risk:

- Paying too much for a property because you don't know enough about the market.
- Taking on more debt than cash flow the property can cover. This can happen when a landlord arranges financing on an unrealistically high monthly rent or fails to factor in a sufficient cushion for repairs and vacancy. Investors who buy and flip or buy, rehab, and sell can see debt payments eat up profits when they don't sell the property as quickly as they hoped to. Incorrectly estimating the costs of repair and rehab also can affect debt and cash flow.
- Renting to bad tenants who fail to pay rent, damage property, and add a tremendous amount of stress to an investor's life.
- Buying and holding in an area where the home values are dropping, or where vandalism and crime are prevalent.
- Incurring liability when buying, selling, or renting by running afoul of fair housing laws, zoning codes, disclosure laws, and other rules and regulations.
- Keeping sloppy books and failing to pay taxes.

You can avoid nearly all of these risks with accurate information about markets, buyers, sellers, rules and regulations, and business practices. In fact, I believe accurate information is the key to profiting in real estate. Disraeli's maxim, "the most successful person in life is the one who has the best information," is relevant to real estate investing. With the right information, you can make sound decisions that make your investment as risk-free as humanly possible. You also can buy property that meets or surpasses the criteria for a good deal, which I'll explain next.

What Is a Good Deal?

To most investors, a good deal is a property that can be purchased for at least 25 to 40 percent below its retail value. I'm ultraconservative by nature and need a cushion. If I'm going to buy a house, fix it up, and sell it, I need—at the very minimum—to buy it at 25 percent below market value. The fact is, 40 percent below is what I'm really looking for. There are two reasons why.

First, I start out with the basic assumption that I will overlook some costs. With almost any piece of property, numerous minor things will go wrong and some hidden repair costs will never be anticipated. Also, some rental property is not easy to sell if, and when, you want to get out. If you have a large enough spread, these problems will not be a major concern.

Second, I enter every deal knowing that real estate can be a risky business. I don't like risk, and I want to avoid risk and any sudden changes in the economy that might otherwise spell financial disaster. I want to grow and enjoy increasing profits. The only way to accomplish my goals is to avoid risk by buying a property at 25 to 40 percent below its retail value, give or take a few points of its value. Only then can I make the kind of money that I'm looking for.

In real estate, you actually make or lose money *when you buy the property.* Buying a property for the right price can overcome almost any marketing obstacle, but a piece of property bought at the wrong price— no matter how you doll it up—can never overcome the handicap of an "off target" purchase price.

You want a deal that lets you sell a property the day after the purchase for more than you bought it. Not every deal that you come across will look good initially, however, negotiated correctly, a deal that once looked bad could turn out to be one of your best. This happens to me all the time. Typically, I'll be presented with a deal that makes no sense whatsoever. Rather than hang up the phone, though, I start asking questions to find out what the seller wants out of the deal. Pretty soon, I start to see the seller's motivating factors and I can come up with a creative way to make the deal work for both of us.

The two most important variables in deciding whether to buy a property are the *projected expenses* and the *projected sales price* (and if you are renting it out, the *projected rental income*). The due diligence you undertake while analyzing a property will help you pinpoint both variables. Information is power, and if you have a lot of information about the property, you will possess a tremendous amount of power and be able to profit handsomely.

 R O B E R T ' S   R U L E S

I usually call or inquire about 40 properties and look at 20 more before I even put a contract down. I want to make sure that I'm getting a good deal. Like any business, real estate investing is a numbers game—you have to do a lot before you make a lot!

Decide Where to Concentrate Your Efforts

Before you begin looking for property, you should decide which area meets your goals. Most successful real estate investors concentrate their efforts in one or two areas. Some investors make a lot of money in high-end neighborhoods, but they only can do a few deals. Others, like myself, choose volume, which is found in lower- and moderate-income areas. Deals are always available, and the demand for affordable housing is strong. In fact, there is a shortage of affordable housing everywhere in the United States today.

Do you want to focus on properties in the central city or in outlying suburbs? Nearby small towns or right down the block? Do you want to focus on single-family homes, multiunit properties, or commercial properties? Answer these questions before you even think about making an offer for a property. For advice, ask other investors how they decided where to concentrate. What areas and properties do they like, and why?

As I've mentioned before, you'll find the best deals in transitional neighborhoods that are just beginning to improve. In many cities, these are older neighborhoods where younger professional people are fixing up houses. Look for homeowners moving in and making repairs, and for evidence that the city is investing money in the area. A steady increase in property values is a good sign. So is an increase in the percentage of houses that are owner occupied as opposed to rentals. A large supply of vacant houses may not be a good indicator.

Keep in mind that good deals are relative. For example, real estate prices in Nashville are low in comparison to prices in urban centers like Chicago, San Francisco, and Miami, but good deals are to be had everywhere. And if a neighborhood is too expensive or doesn't offer any deals, just drive another 30 or 45 minutes. I know there are tremendous opportunities in the hinterlands, the suburbs 45 minutes or farther from the central city. I'd drive 45 minutes to make $14,000—wouldn't you?

Another factor to consider is that local real estate prices reflect the presence of jobs. The more jobs that are created, the more prices go up. When jobs leave, prices go down. Analyze your region very carefully. If your area is declining, you may want to sell what you have rather than hold on to a losing investment—unless it already has hit the bottom and you can see signs of renewal. You can access free data on an area's employment and economy from local real estate agents and chambers of commerce. Request and study the information before selecting an area in which to concentrate.

Every investment requires research. Never invest in anything you don't understand or know well. Research every area thoroughly before you buy. Before you make a purchase, talk to people who know the area. Several times I have found what I thought was a really good deal in an unfamiliar neighborhood, only to learn from someone who knew it—that it was a bad house, a bad deal, and a bad neighborhood. More first-hand evidence of the importance of a strong network!

How to Analyze Properties

To determine the actual value of a property under current market conditions, you must thoroughly research the areas in which it is located. The worksheets and checklists in Appendix A will help you record the results of your investigation and determine whether you've found a truly good deal.

Confirm the Property's Value

It is important to contact your real estate agent, the Registrar of Deeds, or your local tax agency to obtain a list of all the properties that have sold in the previous three to six months in the area that you will be buying. Use these comparable sales, or "comps," to compare the property you are analyzing to similar houses in the neighborhood. Compare the square footage and the selling price to estimate the price per square foot; for example, if the square footage of a somewhat identical home is 1,000 square feet and it sold for $60,000, you can use a price of $60 per square foot as an estimate in your analysis.

Determine If the Property Will Sell

To find out about a property, talk to property managers, the police, religious organizations in the area, and the neighbors. Neighbors know more than almost any professional, because they know the history of the house in question: why its owners are moving, who's getting divorced, who's moving in, what houses in the area sell for, etc.

Also check with the local police to determine if the neighborhood is safe. Safety will have an impact on price and how fast the property gets sold. You also should determine whether it is an area that you feel comfortable traveling in.

Find out how long the property has been on the market. The longer it has been for sale, the more motivated its owner is likely to be. Generally speaking, anything will sell at the right price, and a house that hasn't sold may be overpriced. On the other hand, there may be something wrong with the property, so inspect it closely.

Attending auctions also will confirm the value of a property, so you'll know if you're looking at a solid deal.

If there are five houses in the neighborhood and they're all in the $80,000 range, I suggest you put down $70,000 as an estimate in your projections. This is because there are some neighborhoods where no one buys houses, except for investors. There are other neighborhoods where people buy anything in almost any condition. You need to know this information.

Here's a simple, fail-safe insider system that I use to determine if a property will sell, that is, if it is hot or not, and to avoid spending hard-earned cash on a piece of property that won't work. Prior to buying a property, run an ad in the newspaper describing it. Pretend you're going to rent or sell the property in question. See who calls you. If no one calls, you've learned that the area is dead. Dozens of calls will tell you that you have a potentially very hot property.

Inspect the Property Carefully

It is important to inspect a property carefully to confirm its value and to determine the repair costs required to make it a marketable commodity. The properties you are seeking must have a high profit potential. In almost all cases they will require work in order to yield that profit. Therefore, use a professional appraiser or a home inspector to assess the state of the property, and get bids on repairs from several trustworthy contractors. This is not the time to rely on your own hunches. An error in estimates can cost you dearly. Besides, if a professional inspection uncovers costly, hidden problems, you can show the report and the bids to the seller and ask for a significantly lower price.

Walking through a property with a contractor is one of the most critical phases of analyzing a property. The more times you walk through homes and review expenses, the smarter you get. On the plus side, from time to time you'll also discover assets hidden in the property that will allow you to sell that property a lot quicker than you ever thought. When you're just starting out, I suggest you have at least three contractors walk through the details of a house with you. You'll quickly learn the costs to repair common items of concern such as the central air and heating systems, the cost to paint, the cost to carpet, and so on.

Many new investors like to do the work themselves. But stop and think a minute. How much is your time worth? Is it more economical to pay someone to do it for you, so you can spend more time finding deals, making more money, and spending quality time with your family and friends? If you decide to tackle the work yourself, be sure to include the value of your time when you estimate repair costs.

I always call a certified appraiser or another experienced investor for a professional opinion on the value of the property in unfamiliar neighborhoods where I think I have found a good deal. A quick but professional appraisal of the house will confirm its value and can be shown to potential buyers and/or lenders.

Check the Utilities

Turn on the water, electricity, heat, air-conditioning, and all the appliances when you inspect a property. I once made the mistake of ignoring that advice, and it cost me. The sellers assured me that the plumbing was in great shape, but when I turned on the water after the closing, water shot out of five walls and three ceilings. Many of the pipes were broken. Five thousand dollars later, I had learned my lesson.

Check Zoning Laws

Call your local zoning office to check the zoning laws that apply to the property. They may prevent you from converting a residential property to a more lucrative commercial property—one occupied by a medical, dental, or professional office. And they may not even support the way the property is currently used! You may find that a multiunit building actually is zoned for single-family use, or a property being used for commercial purposes is zoned for residential use. As one investor friend discovered, zoning can turn a potentially great deal into a horrible deal. The $1,500 in rents he planned to get from his recently purchased three-unit building vanished when he discovered that because the building was zoned for single-family use, he legally could collect only $500 a month.

Research the Title

Before you buy any property, you or your attorney should research every deed, trust, or lien recorded against that property to make sure you can insure the title to the property. Title insurance is an insurance policy that guarantees that you have good and clear title to the purchased property. Normally when you buy a property for cash or borrow the money to buy it, the money is used to pay off all of the debt and liens against the property. Title insurance costs vary from state to state. You don't want to buy a property that you can't insure!

You can conduct a simple title search yourself by visiting your local courthouse or Registrar of Deeds. Almost all documents pertaining to the owner or the property are filed in the general index, maintained in binders, on microfiche cards, on computerized printouts, and, increasingly, on the Internet. As noted in Chapter 2, many localities use a filing system called the book and page system, in which property information is recorded in a particular book and on a particular page, which you can find in the general index and then view on a microfiche or computer system.

If your public records search turns up red flags—especially when distressed properties are involved—have a title company or an attorney do a title search and provide you with all the documentation and explanations. In fact, I recommend saving your time and energy and leaving the title search to professionals in the first place. A title search informs you of the chain of title, ownership, and what, if any, liens exist, such as a mortgage, property taxes, and any judgments. Following are some of the red flags you may find that will need to be resolved before you can take title to a property.

Liens and judgments. If your search reveals that the property has a *lis pendens* filed against it, it means that a lien or judgment of some type is pending against the property. This can include almost any type of legal action that has been filed against the property, including an action to obtain money from the property owner for something related to or unrelated to the property. In foreclosure properties, a *lis pendens* filed after the foreclosing trust deed or mortgage will be "extinguished," or canceled, by the foreclosure. But if the *lis pendens* was filed before a foreclosing mortgage, it will not be extinguished at the foreclosure sale. Check to see where the *lis pendens* appears in the pecking order.

Mechanic's liens. Many localities, cities, and states allow contractors, painters, plumbers, and others who work on houses to file a mechanic's lien against a property when they are not paid for their work on a house. A mechanic's lien can sometimes take precedent over all other liens and easily can cloud a title. Therefore, you must make sure that there are no mechanic's liens filed on a property before you become interested in it.

Quitclaim deeds. A quitclaim deed indicates that someone has "quit" his or her interest in the property. When I quitclaim my property to you, that means I give up whatever interest or claim I have on the property. Most states recognize the legality and power of a quitclaim deed; some, like California, have restrictions on them. Check with your attorney or title company for the value of the quitclaim deed.

A quitclaim deed may cause problems with your title company. Because a quitclaim deed is limited in its power, most title companies require or prefer, in order to ensure good title, a grant deed or a warranty deed. A warranty deed means that I warrant this deed to you. Just as your refrigerator comes with a warranty and guarantees, so does this warranty deed. It is a stronger and more powerful form of conveyance or transferring of property, because it warranties and/or guarantees the deed to you.

Tax liens. Tax liens filed by federal, state, or local taxing authorities also may be present. Contact your local tax offices and/or Registrar of Deeds' office to find out what order these liens take on a property in a foreclosure sale. If a lien has been filed, be sure to check on the right of redemption, that is, how long the original owner has the right to redeem, or pay those taxes, and get the property back. Every city, county, and state has a different policy. Some places do not give the previous owners any time at all to redeem their property. Others give the owners up to one full year in which they can pay off their taxes plus interest to get back their property. Many times, the original owner may pay taxes and take back his or her property even after it has been purchased at a tax sale, although the buyer probably will earn interest for the money invested in the property. That rate of interest will vary from state to state and can oftentimes be very high. Call your local Property Tax Assessor's Office or a local title company to find out about the redemption period for local taxes.

Federal tax liens have a 120-day waiting or redemption period. That is, the IRS has 120 days to come in and protect its lien, or it has a 120-day right of redemption. Most title insurance companies will not insure title on a property for 120 days if there is a federal tax lien, because during that time period, the IRS can come in and take over the property. In the case of a foreclosure, the law requires that the government be given a 25-day notice of the sale. If the government is not notified, the lien will not be extinguished with the expiration of the 120-day right of redemption.

 R O B E R T ' S R U L E S

Never buy property without title insurance—you always want to know that there is a clear title to the property that you are buying.

Confirm Your Assumptions with Agents and Lenders

Check your basic assumptions about a location with agents in your region who are familiar with specific areas. Call lenders and ask their views on the area. Use your network to confirm whether the area is undervalued or overvalued, and whether the deal is worth pursuing.

Review Profit and Loss Statements

If the property is an investment property, ask the current owner or property manager for the property's profit and loss statement, or at least a record of the rents, expenses, and taxes. Review the information item by item to understand why the present owner is having financial problems. For example, was it divorce, foreclosure possibilities, poor management, financing difficulties, elderly who want to move out of an area or downgrade their lifestyle, a neighborhood in transition, the owner's lifestyle, unforeseen damage or heavy repair costs, or liens? What is really going on? You need to find out.

Run a Cash Flow Projection

You must run an accurate cash flow projection on every piece of property you intend to buy so that you know what the property is going to cost you. Talk to contractors and other experts in the field. Project the expenses for the appraisal cost, termite letters, surveys, your monthly payments until you sell, property taxes, insurance, utilities, closing costs, commissions, advertising, and finder's fee. In other words, you need to calculate profit and loss projections and every penny that's going to come out of your pocket *before* you do anything with the property. Whether you're planning to buy and hold, buy and flip, or buy, fix, and sell, you need to know exactly what you're getting yourself into.

Explore Financing Options

Check with your local housing authority (HUD, FHA, VA) to see if special financing (for example, a low-interest neighborhood revitalization grant) is available. Plug these numbers into your profit and loss projections.

Consider Who Will Buy the Property

If you buy this property, who will you sell it to? Before you make an offer, ask yourself:

- What kind of person is going to be interested in living here?
- How will I go about finding prospects?
- Do I currently know anyone who would be interested in owning this real estate? (If you do, perhaps you should talk to them first to try and determine their level of interest.)

Stick to Your Guns

Sure, you'll be tempted to buy certain properties in spite of what you discover. Don't do it. Stick with your game plan.

It has been estimated that 98 percent of all real estate purchases are emotional. If you take a businesslike, unemotional approach, you will have an advantage over most buyers and sellers, and you'll make money.

Like a lot of investors, I used to get emotional about property. I didn't like the low- and moderate-income neighborhoods I looked at. While they were decent, I couldn't see myself living there. As a result, I passed up some very good deals. Now, I do real estate by the numbers. I want to know what a property is worth, what I can get it for, and how much I will have to spend on repairs. I'm looking for property to invest in, not live in. It needs to be clean, adequate, and safe. It doesn't have to look like my own home or neighborhood.

Unemotional discipline is the name of the game. A first-rate real estate mind requires a participant/observer outlook: You need to be able to see each deal from your own perspective, *and* from a third-person perspective. Study the market and don't get emotional. If a deal falls through, don't sweat it. There will always be another one.

DON'T BE FRIGHTENED AWAY BY SQUALOR

I'm excited by rundown houses that others have ignored or are avoiding! It's true. I look for houses that are torn up and have broken windows, filthy carpets, holes in floors. Some have five feet of trash in the yard, broken fences, window shades in tatters, broken toilet seats, and poor landscaping. Other potential buyers walk into a poorly maintained house and say, "Oh, no, it'll cost $30,000 to $50,000 to repair this house. It's a pigpen!" That's an emotional response; it's not necessarily logical or true.

Simply walk through the house with a contractor and ask what it will take to turn the poorly maintained home into one in acceptable condition.

Most people think it costs a fortune to repair a house. A good contractor can repair a house and make it look good for a reasonable amount of money. Many ugly properties that you can buy inexpensively just need to be cleaned and painted, and have new floor coverings put in. Find a good contractor who you can work with. Perhaps you may want to find one to be your partner, and they can do the repairs in exchange for part of the profits.

CHAPTER 4

Financing Deals

Some people sit and watch the world go by—and it does.

 —Anonymous

You *can* buy property with no money.

Don't believe it? Well, it's true. You can buy good property without using *any* of your own money. It happens every day. In the past few years, I've bought hundreds of properties without using a penny of my own money. So have many of my students.

To be a successful real estate investor, you need to know how to find good deals *and* how to find the money for these good deals. The sources of funds are almost limitless: You can borrow from banks, mortgage companies, and savings and loans (S&Ls). If you are just starting out, or you have bad credit, you may need to explore alternatives like borrowing from the seller, or partnering with a friend, family member, or other individual interested in a healthy return on his or her investment.

But borrowing money can be risky for the fledgling real estate investor. Every loan *must* be paid back—even loans to friends and family members. Also, making late payments to a financial institution will hurt your credit and, if you can't pay them back at all, you may be forced into bankruptcy. Missing payments to a private investor can be just as damaging, especially if you are trying to build a long-term relationship.

It is best to avoid borrowing money and going into debt when you're just starting out in real estate. I recommend flipping properties, using lease-options, and other techniques that won't tie up your own money and don't require loans from banks. When you've built up enough cash and are more experienced at identifying a truly good deal, you can begin to buy and hold using your own money or by partnering with private investors.

When I first ventured into real estate, I kept my full-time job so I had an income. I saved enough for a down payment, bought a property, and started the cash flow. I always tried to get owner's terms and used cash from properties to buy more properties, and after a few months turned to private investors. I also drew up a business plan, visited several banks repeatedly, and got to know some bankers. Finally, 18 months after I launched my business, a bank opened a credit line for me based on the appraised value of one of my properties. I would use cash from the credit line to purchase a property, and then refinance it with a permanent 15-year mortgage. When I refinanced, I paid off the credit line and would begin to look for another property.

 R O B E R T ' S   R U L E S

Analyze the details of every financing source and make absolutely certain in your cash flow projections that the terms do not place an unbearable burden on your business plan and especially your cash flow.

I took two steps to minimize the risk of borrowing money: I had a cushion of savings in case anything went wrong, and I made absolutely sure I was purchasing a good deal before I incurred any debt.

You need to do the same. A cushion of extra funds is essential. You need enough to handle three to six months of debts on your household and business. If your monthly expenses are $3,000, you'll want to have $18,000 in cash reserve.

You also need to protect yourself by buying a property the right way and making sure it is a good, solid deal you can sell quickly and at a profit if you have to. This is the best possible way to reduce risk and prevent problems with dcbt.

This chapter will examine three ways to finance a real estate deal:

1. Bank financing
2. Partnerships with private investors
3. Seller financing

Bank Financing

Borrowing money from a bank is often a catch-22 situation. Banks require that you have a track record, a good credit history, and the ability to put up some of your own money—requirements that many beginning investors simply cannot meet.

Nevertheless, it is quite possible to borrow money from a bank. If you have cstablished a good relationship with a bank and have a decent credit history, you should be able to find a bank to lend you money. The secret is to be prepared. Lenders want organized data. They want to know who you are and what you're buying. They're going to want tax returns, financial statements, and a detailed analysis of the property. They want to be assured that the risk is low, and they want to know what the market value will be once it has been renovated, what the property will rent for (if you'll be renting it out), what the vacancy and repair expenses will be, and what you expect to nct.

Start your quest for financing by developing a personal and long-term relationship with at least two bankers who handle real estate loans. Take them to lunch. Show them your business plan and let them know your personal philosophy. Ask their advice. Say something like, "I respect your opinion and position and would like your opinion on this deal." If they won't lend to you, ask for referrals to other lenders or ask what it would take for them to lend to you. Keep in touch, and eventually you may secure your loan. Persistence is the mark of success in financing as well as business. Even people who have bad credit will get financing if they stick with it. If I had quit the first three times I heard "no" from the bank, I wouldn't be where I am today.

When I talk to a bank or mortgage company, I never directly ask for a loan. That immediately throws up a wall and puts a banker on the defensive! A more oblique approach lets the banker relax and look at your project objectively. I describe my business, explain what I'm planning to do next, and ask for the banker's opinion about the project. "Would you know anybody that might one day finance this project?" is one of my favorite questions. The worst the banker can do is refer you elsewhere, but you might be told that this is just the kind of project the bank is looking to finance. Feedback from bankers is always helpful; if they see a flaw in your thinking or suggest a better way to structure your business, listen. Follow their advice and come back with a plan that incorporates their suggestions.

Remember that the primary objective of a bank, credit union, or S&L is to make safe and secure loans. The more supporting documents you provide, the more you convince them that lending to you is a solid proposition. Pull them together in an organized fashion and you can prepare a powerful financing package that will knock their socks off. (See the next section for a discussion of the financing package.) Provide the bank with "more than they want to know" about your potential investment in the form of an in-depth business plan for the property you intend to purchase.

Keep in mind that banks are under tremendous pressure to provide Community Reinvestment Act (CRA) money, which requires them to invest money in low-income neighborhoods in order to get credit from the federal government. That is, they provide money to low-income families that will be used for affordable housing. This gives banks an incentive and a willingness to expend money and take more risk to renovate specific neighborhoods. One of your projects just may qualify.

Compare the interest rates you are offered with other financial institutions in your area. Remember: Everything is negotiable. Everything. That includes interest rates, points, fees, and terms. Check the terms of every loan agreement you are offered—not only the interest payments, the insurance, the balloon, and any escape clauses (that allow the lender to escape from the low interest rates they've offered), but every detail in the contract, including the penalty if you cannot make a payment.

The best way to negotiate is to let the bank know that other institutions are interested in loaning you money. Play the banks and mortgage companies against each other. Let each institution know that you are "shopping"—talking with two or three lenders. Say, "Yes, I've been led to believe that I will get the loan I'm seeking. I'm just trying to see if I can get a better deal from someone else." It's amazing what a little competition will do.

Once you have a bank loan, call your banker at least once a month and remind him or her that your disciplined and detailed business plan is in operation and progressing smoothly and that you are limiting the use of their money for the single purpose intended in your business plan. Banks rarely hear from their customers, so they'll appreciate the professionalism that you bring to the deal.

 R O B E R T ' S   R U L E S

The best way to ensure that you can make payments on debt is to avoid having numerous credit lines. Bankers live by the 28:34 rule: Mortgage payments, including real estate taxes, should be approximately 28 percent of an individual's gross monthly salary, with no more than 34 percent of their gross salary per month spent on all other debts.

Design a Successful Financing Package

The key to obtaining financing from a bank or a private partner is to prepare a professional, organized financing package that includes a detailed business plan, which explains exactly what you are planning to do and anticipates every question that a lender might want answered. Because most people approach lending institutions without a financing package, a professional looking package will set you apart from your competition. Have an accountant review the numbers and recommend improvements to the package. Make your package look professional: neatly typed, well-organized, illustrated with pictures, and bound in a binder or folder. (Some of the components of a financing package can be found in Appendix B.)

Your financing package should include the following:

- A nice title page:
   Loan Request for Joe Buyer
   Presented to the First Bank of Nashville

- A mission statement:

    To profitably buy, rehabilitate, and sell homes in (your city) that will benefit the community and provide much-needed, quality, affordable housing to first-time home-buyers.
- A brief, professional-sounding, short- and long-term business plan that is one to two pages long
- Your résumé
- Your financial statement
- A description of the property you want to borrow against
- Details of your loan request
- A picture of the property you want to buy and a map showing its location
- A copy of your credit report (request one from your local credit-reporting agency)
- Two years of your tax returns
- An executive summary of you and your loan request, stressing benefits to the bank
- At least six references
- Cash flow projections and analysis
- Projected return on investment (ROI)
- Information detailing the demand for the investment property
- A list of your past successes in converting homes and income-expense statements on each property (Include before and after pictures of other houses you may have renovated.)

Before your bank will lend you money, it also will want to see the following:

- An appraisal of the property
- An accurate survey report
- A termite report
- Results of tests of wells and septic tanks
- Proper title, liability, and property and casualty insurance

Types of Mortgages

When I finance a deal through a bank, I get a 15- or 30-year fixed-rate mortgage. If I'm planning to buy and hold, I prefer a 30-year fixed loan so my monthly payment will remain the same even as rents increase. Also, if my ROI will be 40 or 50 percent and I can borrow at 10 percent, a long-term loan is very desirable.

Some investors argue that you can save money and get out of debt faster with a 15-year loan. I think you're better off making extra payments on a 30-year loan than locking yourself into the higher payments required for a 10- or 15-year mortgage. Remember, you must pay the bank whether the economy is weak or strong!

Here is a quick summary of other mortgages available from lending institutions:

Blanket mortgage. A blanket mortgage covers all or more than one of your properties and allows you to use equity as collateral on new financing. If you are having trouble getting qualified and you have other assets, this could allow you to obtain a new mortgage. The caveat: You put your collateralized equity—in other words, your properties—at risk.

Graduated payment mortgage (GPM). A GPM is a mortgage with reduced payments initially and higher future payments on a predetermined schedule. The payment then levels off for the remainder of the 15- or 30-year contract. GPMs are great if you want more property for your money and you are certain your income will increase over the years. Another benefit is that a GPM makes it easier to qualify for a larger loan, because first-year payments are lower. However, negative amortization can occur. Because the interest you are saving is added to your mortgage, you could end up owing a lot more than a simple mortgage would have been. Negative amortization loans are rare, but you should at least know they exist.

Graduated payment adjustable mortgage (GPAM). Like a GPM mortgage, GPAM payments are reduced initially and gradually increase over regular intervals. Interest rates, however, are adjusted on 3-, 4-, or 5-year intervals. This allows the borrower to make lower payments for a specified number of years and then to accelerate the principal.

Pledged account mortgage. A pledged account mortgage is similar to the GPAM above, except that the buyer is required to make a substantial down payment (10 percent to 15 percent), which is then deposited to a pledged savings account.

Adjustable- or variable-rate mortgage. Adjustable- or variable-rate mortgage payments are indexed to current interest rates and the loan interest rate is adjusted at least once a year. This is great if interest rates are dropping—but if they increase, so will payments.

Shared appreciation mortgage. A shared appreciation mortgage provides a repayment schedule in which you choose to share any profit (equity appreciation) in the property with the lender when it is sold. In return, the lender will reduce your interest rate below market, and therefore reduce your payment. This is for those who want lower interest rates (and payments) or cannot qualify at existing interest rates. The problem is, that as a buyer, you will be giving up a portion of your ROI when you sell the property, typically at a specified date.

Rollover mortgage (ROM). In a ROM, the borrower and the lender agree to a repayment term of perhaps 15 or 30 years, during which the mortgage rate is renegotiated or rolled over at regular intervals. This is great for the lender if interest rates increase, and the buyer always can refinance.

Renegotiable rate mortgage (RRM). An RPM is renewed at short intervals and interest rates are adjusted to an index. Maximum yearly adjustment is generally .005 (one-half of one) percent per year over a 15- or 30-year schedule. This instrument is for those who believe interest rates *will* head downward.

Federal Housing Administration (FHA) loan. The FHA insures mortgages, it doesn't lend money. If you take an FHA loan from an S&L, the government insures your mortgage payment to the lender. Most FHA loans are fully assumable if the buyer can qualify. There are no prepayment penalties; but the buyer and the property must qualify for the FHA loan. There is a maximum loan amount, and the borrower must occupy the property and pay a mortgage insurance premium.

Department of Veterans Affairs (VA) mortgage. A VA mortgage is essentially the same as the FHA program, with the important distinction being that the borrower does not have to come up with a down payment.

Working with Private Investors

Most financial institutions require a borrower to personally guarantee every loan and to comply with very stringent credit and paperwork requirements. I know many real estate investors who own hundreds of properties and have never borrowed any money from a bank. They also have never personally guaranteed any loan. That's because they turn to partners or private investors who lend on the property without requiring a personal guarantee.

There are advantages and disadvantages to borrowing from private investors. On the upside, you often can bypass a bank's stringent asset and income requirements and lower or eliminate your liability and risk. However, when you borrow from private investors or lenders, you pay a higher interest rate, and therefore must give up more of your profit.

If you have little or no money, you probably need to start with partners and/or investors. Relatives, friends, employers, and retirees seeking higher returns on their money all may be good sources of money. When you find a property that is a good deal, draw up a business plan for it and present it to anyone and everyone who could help you. Perhaps you can help someone who is only earning 5 to 6 percent on their money in savings accounts, certificates of deposit, bonds, etc., to make 9 or even 10 percent instead. If you are finding truly undervalued properties, then you can offer your investors a very safe first mortgage. Example: If the property you found has a retail value of $60,000 and you can buy it and fix it up for a total cost of $40,000 *and* you can prove to your investors that this is true (using sales of similar houses in the neighborhood and comparing them to yours), you can offer them an extremely safe mortgage with an equity cushion of $20,000. Many very successful real estate entrepreneurs began this way. Some investors I know of have raised hundreds of thousands of dollars, and some have even raised millions over the years.

Because you found the deal and you're going to do all of the work to ensure the deal gets done, make an offer to your partner that if he or she will put up the money, you will split the profits 50/50. Your offer might sound like this:

> Mary, I found a property that I can buy for $20,000. I'll spend $5,000 fixing it up, and then sell it for $45,000. What I need from you is a loan to buy the property, which will be secured by a first mortgage. I'll oversee everything and we'll

split the profits. The work should be completed within 45 to 60 days and I should be able to sell the property within two to three months after that for $45,000. That's a $20,000 gain, of which you will receive $10,000. That's a 50 percent return on your money in less than five months.

If you don't know anybody who has this type of money, you'll need to start networking with accountants, lawyers, retirees, investment advisors, and older real estate entrepreneurs (who simply don't have the time to keep running around finding deals). Another possibility is to develop joint-venture relationships with contractors, nonprofit organizations, or church groups. You also can find investors by advertising in newspapers using ads like the following:

Earn up to 12% on your money!
Very secure investment.
Call or write for more information.
Real and safe!
[Your phone number and address]

Don't let the banks make all the money!
Earn a high rate of return on your money,
secured by valuable real estate.
Call now.
[Your phone number]

Always pay your investors back 100 percent of their investment money first. By paying the investors back their initial investment before any profits are split up, you'll make them happy to do business with you again. If there is a profit on the house, then split it up and pay them quickly.

If you work with partners or investors, always pay them more than they expect. Look at it from the investor's viewpoint. If you promise the investor 10 percent on his money and then you pay him 11 or 12 percent, explaining that you made so much money on this deal you wanted to share it, do you think he'll want to do business with you again? Of course he will! And repeat business is what you're after, not the one-time killing. If you flip or rehab a property and make $15,000 once you sell it, why not give the investor an extra $1,000 after your 50/50 split?

Tell him it's a "kicker," or a bonus for working with you. And if you break down the return on his money over a 12-month period, I think he'll be glad to do business with you again. He even may tell his friends, relatives, and business partners to lend money to you.

Take every measure to make sure your first deal goes well. Most important, make absolutely sure it is a good deal by doing the following:

- Estimate rehab and acquisition costs as accurately as possible.
- Analyze each deal and write it up.
- Put in contingencies.
- Be conservative.

You want to make your investor as happy as possible. When you have developed a pool of investors and prospective investors, send them a one- or two-page monthly newsletter that brings them up to date on your activities and explains the life of your investments, the tax consequences, leasing, and so on.

 R O B E R T ' S   R U L E S

I try to take on partners for specific transactions only—property by property or deal by deal. I always consult an attorney to write up an agreement that specifies duties and responsibilities, and includes a way for one partner to buy out the other and leave the partnership. It's also possible to form a corporation with your partner and have that corporation own the property acquired with the money. Always consult an attorney to find the best way to get your arrangement on paper.

Seller Financing

If you can't get the funds you're looking for from a bank, some sellers—generally sellers who are desperate for a buyer, or who have little or no balance on the property—*will* give you financing. This is often an excellent situation if you are the buyer, because no outside lender is required and you do not have to qualify or put down a large cash payment. In some cases a buyer also can obtain better terms and interest rates simply because the owner is anxious to sell in a slow market.

Always ask for seller financing (also called owner's terms) before you seek any other type of financing arrangement. Be creative. For example, you can offer to fix up a property that needs work and share the profits with the seller when the property is sold. That is, if you get a contract for $40,000 on the house, put $5,000 into fixing it up, and then sell it for $60,000, both you and the seller will be happy dividing up the profits. Many new investors get started this way.

While almost all sellers will say that they want cash, it is possible to obtain owner's terms if you can negotiate. If sellers demand cash, ask them why. Usually they will tell you. Ask what their plans are for the cash. If they need to pay off a small debt, then ask what they are going to do with the remainder. If they tell you that they are going to invest it, ask how much they plan to make on their money. Perhaps they can earn 6 to 8 percent. Your response to this would be: "How would you like to pay off your debt and earn 9 to 10 percent with a safe investment?" They should be interested because it meets their needs. You then can offer them $3,000 cash down with owner's terms for the balance over 20, 25, or 30 years at 9 or 10 percent interest. If you don't have good credit, it's the easiest way to get financing. Even if you have good credit, you'll probably end up with a better deal on owner's terms.

Assumable Loans and Mortgages

Assuming an existing loan or mortgage is another type of owner's terms. Loans that can be assumed by anyone are like gold, but they're not easy to uncover.

If you find a property with an older loan on it, or one with seller financing, get a copy of the actual loan agreements. If the loan is assumable, then anyone can sign on and take over the payments, if it is non-qualifying. For example, you may find a house valued at $150,000 that has a 15-year loan on it with a balance of $95,000. You could buy the house and just take over the payments without having to qualify for a new loan. (If the seller wants $120,000 for the house, you will need to come up with the $25,000 difference—perhaps by taking out a second mortgage on the property.)

Many new loans also are qualifying assumable loans. That is, you may be able to take over the loan after you apply and qualify with the bank or mortgage company that has the original loan. When you assume a loan, you assume the responsibility for the payments (the difference between the sales price and the balance owed) on the seller's existing mortgage. This is the way to go if you have available cash and want to benefit from a lower interest rate as well as avoid closing costs. Another plus is that under this scenario you may not have to qualify, although some lenders may still require a buyer to qualify. Lenders also can increase your interest rate on the assumption. (There is no need to qualify on FHA or VA assumable mortgages, nor will these agencies boost interest rates.) Be aware that a seller with a low interest rate can ask a higher price for the property. You should note, however, that many pre-1986 mortgages are assumable nonqualifying; post-1986 mortgages are mostly qualifying assumable or are not assumable.

Most mortgages have a due-on-sale clause that entitles the bank to call in the loan if the property is sold. In this case, get written permission allowing you to take over the property so that the due-on-sale clause will not be exercised by the bank. Some banks may give you this permission to take over the mortgage, but make sure you get this permission in writing.

Some investors ignore the due-on-sale clause. They make payments directly to the seller, who remains on the first mortgage. It is very unlikely the mortgage company will discover the sale as long as it keeps receiving payments from the original borrower. This is not illegal in most states, but the bank or mortgage company could discover there was a "sell" and call in the loan. That means the entire mortgage or loan becomes due, and you must sell the property for enough cash to pay off the loan, or quickly refinance it. Also, the credit rating of the original seller, still listed on the mortgage, is at risk; if the original loan is not paid off, he or she could be liable.

Another way to get around the due-on-sale clause is to lease-option the property. Let's say the house is valued at $200,000 and has a $150,000 mortgage on it, with a payment of $1,400 per month due. If you cannot assume the loan, than you could lease it for ten years at $1,400 per month with a ten-year option to buy it anytime you wanted for $150,000 or the loan amount, whichever is lower. The $1,400 lease payment goes toward paying the mortgage. After five years, the house would be worth more than $200,000 and the mortgage would have gone down with each monthly mortgage payment. Perhaps you could lease it to a tenant for $1,700 per month while you pay only $1,400. The option gives you the exclusive right to buy the property anytime during the life of the option. While a lease-option usually will not trigger a due-on-sale clause, you or your attorney must review the original loan document to make sure.

Wraparound Mortgages

Also called an all-inclusive mortgage (AIM) or an all-inclusive trust deed (AITD), a "wraparound mortgage" allows the buyer to take title to a property by combining a first mortgage and a second, or "wrap," that includes the first. For safety's sake (because the seller will know precisely when a buyer stops making payments), the seller can keep the first mortgage and make payments from the monies paid on the wrap. The wrap frequently is used on FHA or VA mortgages, but many lenders will not allow a wrap because they require a clause in the contract stipulating a continual interest rate escalator. Some secondary lenders also prohibit wraps.

A wrap can give you an opportunity to purchase a property at a lower interest rate than the current market, and gives the seller an additional safeguard against nonpayment. In addition, the seller can earn more money due to the difference in interest rates after the property is sold.

Here's an example: Joe owns a house with one 30-year mortgage for $60,000 on it. He has been making monthly payments of $600 for seven years. You negotiate with Joe to buy his house for $1,000 down, and you make the $600 payment to the bank. You have three choices in paying the bank (the first mortgage holder). If you pay the bank directly, Joe has to worry about whether you are making payments. If you pay Joe directly and rely on him to pay the bank, you risk nonpayment by Joe. A third option is to contract with a third party—an attorney or trustee—to make the payments to the bank.

You next sell the house to Sue for $3,000 down and payments of $800 per month for 30 years, an approximate total cost of $78,000. You then wrap the first mortgage; that is, Sue sends you $800 each month, you send Joe (or his mortgage company) $600 each month, and you keep the $200-per-month difference as your profit. Title passes to the new buyer, whose mortgage is wrapped around the first one. Always consult with a real estate attorney before you get involved with a wrap.

Contract for Deed

A contract for deed is very similar to a wraparound mortgage. Normally, if you pay cash for a house and get a new loan, you get both the title and the deed to the property. In a contract for deed, also called a contract for sale or a land contract, the seller retains the title to the property until the buyer meets the complete terms of the contract. The buyer has to provide a down payment on the property and pay the monthly balance. This is excellent if you want to leverage your cash or if you can't qualify for a loan.

A contract for deed states that you get the deed (basically, the title) after you perform a contract. So if there is a house worth $200,000 with a $150,000 mortgage or loan on it and payments of $1,500 per month for 15 years, then you could have a contract for deed drawn up that states that you will pay the $1,500 per month for the 15 years, and when the loan is paid off and you performed your contract to pay, then you get the deed.

The first mortgage loan is still on the property. With a contract for deed for the property, it is yours to sell, rent, or contract-for-deed it to someone else. Your contract for deed could be subject to the first mortgage loan, and the seller could fail to deliver a clear title by defaulting on the loan or because of a divorce, tax lien, etc. Use a third party such as an attorney, certified public accountant, or friend to make sure all of the taxes and insurance are paid.

Other Options for Borrowing Money

Here's a quick summary of ways to borrow money, though not all are recommended:

- *Equity lines.* You can use the equity in your house to borrow money to begin, but I don't recommend it. While these loans can be very attractive, you are using your house as collateral and could lose it if a deal goes sour. Be careful: You don't want to lose your house.
- *Finance companies.* Finance companies often charge higher than normal interest rates, and it's easy to get in over your head. This is the choice of last resort!
- *Government grants.* Some government programs will lend money to repair low- and moderate-income properties or properties in a certain area. These are not mortgages, but getting one of

these grants means you do not have to borrow money for repairs. Contact your local housing authority to determine how the Department of Housing and Urban Development (HUD) and other government grant programs function, and how you can qualify. HUD information also is included at my Web site, <www.shemin .com>.

- *Credit cards.* You can use your credit cards to borrow money. Interest rates are exorbitant, but if you are certain you can flip a property quickly prior to closing, you may want to risk it. Once, when I needed quick cash, I bought and sold a property within three weeks, paid off the credit card—and got enough frequent flyer miles for a free airline ticket. Also, I use a very low-interest credit card. I only recommend this *very* risky strategy for very experienced investors who can count on a deal and can pay back the money.

- *Cash value in life insurance.* If a life insurance policy has been in existence for six years or longer, you may be able to qualify for a low interest rate loan that you will pay back to your policy. Check with your insurance carrier for details and guidelines about borrowing your cash value.

- *Money from a brokerage house.* If you own stocks, bonds, or any other marketable security, you can borrow money from a brokerage house on those securities for as little as prime rate plus 1 percent or even at prime. Someone with securities also can borrow the money from their brokerage house and lend it to you for 4 or 5 percent more. Secure the loan with a first mortgage and fix up, sell, or rent, the property. Make sure the investor understands that the stocks and bonds must be used to pay the brokerage back if you default. By the way, someone with a self-directed individual retirement account can make the same arrangement and earn interest tax-free.

- *Second mortgage.* You also can take out a second mortgage on your own home—an excellent instrument if you lack sufficient cash to buy a property, if interest rates are too high or hard to get, or if you want to purchase a higher priced property from a motivated owner. Second mortgage holders often receive a higher rate of interest because, in the event of a default, a second mortgage is junior (or second) to another senior (or first) mortgage that has first repayment right to an outstanding balance. The term of the loan is also shorter, so payments could be larger. Second mortgages frequently are not permissible on FHA loans or on high-percentage financing arrangements (that is, on homes whose existing loans are 65 percent or more of their value).

No Money Down—Difficult, yet Possible

It is possible, in negotiating seller financing, to convince the seller to sell you a property with no money down and payments to be made monthly.

Let's say you find a home that you think is worth $75,000. You negotiate to buy it for $50,000, with no cash at closing. The seller will pay all closing costs, and you will pay $500 a month for 20 years. Sounds great, doesn't it? Well, the seller would have to be pretty motivated to take a deal like this. Nevertheless, I've seen it happen.

If the house needs work, explain to the seller that you are going to spend time and money repairing the house—this is like a down payment. Your time and your money are going into the house so that the seller has little risk. In the event that you do not make payments to the seller, the seller gets to take back a home that is much more valuable because you just fixed it up.

In negotiating owner's terms, always ask for the payments to begin as late as possible, with the first payment due in one year, three months, or at the end of the first month. If you are buying the house to rent it out, you can use the first month's rent to pay down your payments to the seller.

The following are a number of creative ways to come up with a down payment if the owner insists on one.

Barter. You can offer to barter goods or services with the owner for the down payment on the property. If you manufacture an item such as furniture or a boat, you can offer a direct exchange of your goods as a down payment. Just make sure you trade for retail value. You can also issue a credit to the seller for an unlimited time.

Pay the down payment in installments. You can ask the seller to agree to let you pay the down payment on terms. If you find a seller who wants $10,000 down on a $100,000 property that is a great deal, you can offer $11,000, but only if you can pay it over 30, 20, 10, 5, 2, or 1 year.

Use the real estate agent's commission. If the seller wants six to ten percent down at closing, negotiate with the agent to take the commission over time. At the closing, the seller generally has to pay the commission in cash to the agent. If the agent agrees to take the commission in the form of a promissory note (although it isn't very likely), this saves the seller some cash at closing, which can go toward the down payment. In other words, the agent gives his or her 6 percent commission to the seller, and you give the agent a note promising to pay the commission over a certain period of time. This is rare, but I've seen it happen.

Assume the seller's obligations. Instead of making a cash down payment, assume some of the seller's notes and/or obligations. If the seller has a payment due, offer to make the payment yourself as your down payment.

Sell off part of the property. If you are buying a group of properties or land, sell off part of the land or properties for more than you have optioned or contracted for and use the proceeds from that sale to make the down payment. For example, you are buying four houses for $30,000 per house. You know that they are worth more. You negotiate 60 days to close and you need 10 percent cash down at closing. You flip one of the houses for $50,000 to someone else. At the simultaneous closings, you make your down payment from the $20,000 proceeds you just received on the flip. Yes, it can be done!

Partner a deal with a private investor. If you find a property that is a great deal and you need 10 percent down to close, persuade a friend or an investor to partner with you. Say that if your partner puts 10 percent down on the property, then you'll split the profits 50/50 when you flip the house.

Let's say you find an apartment building that is valued at $250,000 for sale at $150,000. The seller wants 10 percent down and will carry a note for 20 years at a 10 percent interest rate (approximate payments would be $1,300 per month). The apartment building has ten units, and each one will rent, on average, for about $450 per month (or $4,500 per month total). You can make $3,200 per month (before some expenses, of course), but you don't have the down payment. Ask a friend or an investor for the $15,000 down payment and offer to make your friend a 50 percent partner on the deal. In ten months' time, your partner will make back his or her down payment, and you'll be making $1,600 per month and building equity—without ever putting up a dime!

Joint venture with the seller. Convince a motivated seller to let you help sell his or her property for a fee, or split the profit. Let's say the property is worth $200,000 but the motivated seller will take $160,000 so he or she can move out of state. You can agree in writing that—if you are able to sell the property for anything more than $160,000 in the next 90 days—you will split 50/50 on all monies above $160,000. So if you sell it for $190,000, you will make $15,000 and the seller will get $15,000 more than he or she initially would have received.

You don't need to be a real estate broker with access to the Multiple Listing Service to sell the house. Signs, ads, and listings on the many FSBO Web sites can be very effective. (For more ideas, see Chapter 6.)

Lease-option agreement. The lease-option agreement, described in Chapter 1, also can help you acquire a property without cash. It is also an easy way to sidestep a due-on-sale clause, which makes an assumable mortgage due and payable on sale. The seller benefits because he or she no longer needs to be concerned with mortgage payments. Generally, the sellers can ask for a higher price for the property and get it. After all, the house will be worth more when the buyer exercises the option, so a house that might sell for $100,000 right now can be optioned for $110,000—still a good deal for the buyer if prices rise steadily. The downside for the sellers, however, is that they don't receive their money until the sales contract takes effect.

CHAPTER 5

Controlling, Holding, and Protecting Real Estate

History records the success of men with objective and a sense of direction. Oblivion is the position of small men overwhelmed by obstacles.

−William H. Danforth

Not long ago, one of my favorite bird dogs told me he had found a really great deal on a house on which the mortgage company had fore-closed. The mortgage company only wanted to reclaim its loan balance out of the sale and was selling the property for $70,000, even though it was worth at least $120,000. It sounded too good to be true!

We went and looked at the house—a spacious, modern, and well-maintained four-bedroom, three-bath home on almost an acre of land. It had a pool and a full garage, and needed nothing more than interior paint and some new carpet. It was surrounded by beautiful homes in the $130,000 to $180,000 range. It sure looked like a good deal, but because I was not very familiar with the area, I decided to do some more research on the property. Although the bird dog had brought me comparable listings showing that similar houses in that area sold for $130,000 to $150,000, and the tax assessor had appraised the house at $135,000, I still was not sure. A few days later, when I had verified everything I had been told, I found out that the house had been sold the day that I had looked at it for about $70,000.

That day, I relearned one of the first rules of real estate: "He who hesitates loses." I hesitated and I lost. When I first looked at the house and thought it was a good deal, I should have locked it up immediately. That is, I should have put a contract on the house to control it. But because I didn't put a contract on it, I had no control of the house and it was sold to someone who probably profited greatly from the property.

Once you find a good deal, you must "lock up" the property as quickly as possible. An oral agreement with a seller who says you can have it at your price means nothing—until the deal is in writing. Controlling or locking up a property means you have the property under some type of written contract—for example, a signed purchase agreement or an option contract. Neither a purchase agreement nor an option contract convey title to you. These contracts simply state that the seller will transfer title to you on a future date, so long as both you and the seller meet the specifications spelled out in the contract. This allows you to control that real estate for as long as the time period or limitations of your contract specify. If you "control" it, the seller cannot sell the property out from under you. You, on the other hand, can resell the property prior to the closing date.

Controlling property is the first step in purchasing and profiting from real estate. You also need to know how to hold a property—that is, to determine what name should appear on the title—and how to protect it by purchasing adequate insurance against loss and liability. Controlling, holding, and protecting are the subjects of this chapter.

How to Negotiate a Contract and Control Property

Let's say you've found what you think might be a great property. What should you do? First, you need to lock it up. If you don't put a contract on a property immediately, someone else will. Without a contract or an option to buy, the seller is able to sell the property to someone else. (Sample contracts and option agreements are located in Appendix C.)

Negotiating a contract is really negotiating a deal. In my view, the most important thing about negotiating contracts—and the best way to ensure that the final deal is very favorable—is to understand what it is that the seller really wants or needs. I call this the "Game of 1,000 Polite

Questions." Try to get answers to the following questions. Be sure to phrase them in a way that is appropriate and nonthreatening.

- Why are the sellers selling?
- What are they going to do with the money?
- Why do they need the money?
- What are their real reasons for getting rid of the house?
- How long have they owned the property?
- Who actually owns it (is it in their name or someone else's name or owned by a partnership)?
- Is there a time frame in which they must sell the property?
- How quickly do they want to sell it?
- How long have they been trying to sell it?
- How have they tried to sell it?
- What will happen to the property if they don't sell it?
- Is the owner in financial trouble?
- What type of neighborhood is the property in?
- Is there a mortgage on the property?
- Is the mortgage assumable?
- Will they take owner's terms?
- If they do not want owner's terms and insist on cash, what are they going to do with the cash? Perhaps their answer to this question can help you. Maybe they are going to invest it to get a 9 percent return, often even 10 percent—that is, owner's terms!

Recently I found a newspaper ad listing eight houses for sale that included the phrase "Owner financing possible, call." I immediately called the seller and asked a lot of questions including where the properties were, how much they were renting for, and what kind of financing was being offered. The seller was offering 20 percent down and a note for 20 years at 8 percent interest. The eight houses, which averaged about $31,000 apiece, were a mixed bag of properties that included two duplexes, some single-family houses, and two houses with rather large tracts of land. All were in pretty good shape, all were rented, and the properties were receiving a positive cash flow. Obviously, this seemed to be a very good deal.

Over lunch, I talked to the seller and asked my 1,000 questions. In my mind, I was very happy to offer the price that he was asking; and he told me (and I knew it was true) that there were many other people interested in this property. He felt very comfortable with me and my ability

☞ R O B E R T ' S   R U L E S

Try to include as many of the following items as possible in your contract with a seller. You may not always get them—but if you don't ask, you'll never know. And the more you ask for, the more you'll get!

- If you get owner's terms, ask that no payments be due for one year or at the very least six months.

- Ask to put nothing down.

- If seller demands a down payment, offer as little as possible.

- Ask for a below-market interest rate and long-term 30- or 35-year mortgage.

- Ask for the mortgage to be assumable and that it can be subordinated.

- If owner financing is available, attempt to avoid personal liability on mortgages and notes. It's unlikely the sellers will agree to this, but you might as well ask.

- If it is a rental property, ask for the rent to be included in your purchase price, so that you get credit for the next two or three months before the closing. That is, you get credited with three months' rent, while it remains the seller's duty to collect all rent.

- Require that everything stay with the property—carpet, drapes, window treatments, appliances, air conditioners, etc.

- Tell the seller you would like to close as late as possible. If you are going to flip the property, a late closing gives you more than enough time to find another buyer, not to mention time to think about the purchase, inspect the house, and conduct a thorough title search.

ROBERT'S RULES

(continued)

- Ask the seller to pay all the closing costs and the cost of title insurance.

- Ask the seller to provide a "termite letter" guaranteeing that there is no termite damage. If there is termite damage, the seller should pay for correcting it.

- Ask the seller to pay for repairs and/or upgrades, or at least give you credit off the purchase price for those repairs.

to actually close on the properties and manage them so he wouldn't have to take them back (a fear of all sellers who are taking owner's terms).

As I asked questions, it became apparent that he had inherited the properties through an estate settlement. He did not enjoy managing properties, he was not making money at it, he was not good at it, he had another job that took up a lot of time, and he didn't want to spend his time worrying about the properties. The main reason he wanted to sell them was that there was a $50,000 debt on the properties, as well as a $1,088 note due every month. When I uncovered this information, I offered him exactly what he wanted—to take over the note and pay him enough to pay off the debt. The end result: I got the property at a much lower price than I had originally anticipated (about $18,000 a house instead of $31,000). By asking questions and finding out the seller's true motivation—to pay off some debt and get rid of what he considered to be a big headache—I was able to give the seller what he wanted and I got a much better deal.

Never assume that you know the answers to these questions. You might be very surprised by what you learn during your conversation! What you find out will help you in every subsequent step of negotiations.

Your questions should determine exactly how motivated a seller is to "unload" the property. If you do not have a motivated seller, you probably do not have a good deal. Use the answers to draft an action plan that keys in on the personal needs and objectives of the seller. It is critical that you know how the seller will personally win by getting the results that you can deliver.

 ROBERT'S RULES

Negotiating Price

Always offer the lowest price possible, because every dollar off the purchase price is a dollar that you save. Remember, you make money in real estate when you buy a piece of property. Some people routinely offer very low prices for property they want to buy. They may offer $10,000 or $15,000 on a property listed at $40,000 just to see if the seller will take the bait. Most won't, but if you make enough of these offers, someone might accept one. Never hesitate or feel timid about making a low offer, even to an agent. The agent may laugh and look at you funny, but it's the agent's true (and *only*) job to carry the offer, no matter how ludicrous, to the seller.

Throughout your negotiations, continue to ask questions that are geared to solving the seller's personal or financial problem. Your goal is to get below the tip of the iceberg to the solution at hand. Questions also will help you determine how receptive the seller is to the "What if I could give you X in cash today? What is your downside limit?" approach. If you stay with statements such as, "The data show such and such," or "Our strategic analysis shows the following," then the data become the disinterested third party, and personality conflict is eliminated. Thus, your current position and the seller's specific objectives can be better accomplished while untenable positions are eliminated.

Determine the "red flags" that could kill the deal, and reduce or eliminate them in advance. For example, does the seller actually own the property? What is the actual debt on the property? If it's worth $100,000 and has a $90,000 mortgage or note, the owner will not be motivated to sell for any less.

Establish an early win/win financial strategy so that the seller quickly can see you as a partner in his or her success rather than as an opponent to be overcome. This is a key element in the sale: When you know the seller's needs, tailor a strategy to meet them. If the seller offers resistance, tells you that certain information is private, or just won't divulge something, say, "I'm here to help you, but if you won't tell me the information I need, then I cannot help. Let me assure you that if I cannot help you, I'll let you know immediately and I will try to find someone else who can." It's a lot like going to the doctor. You've got to be candid about your symptoms before the doctor can devise a treatment plan!

Be tentative about suggesting strategies until you know all the facts. Use conditional language, like "We *may* be able to get you the cash you need to get out of the house quickly like you want to." Don't promise anything until you have uncovered all the information you need.

Take an efficient and professional approach to negotiations and try to seek out everyone's actual position in the selling decision. Be persistent, but never be forceful or overbearing. The seller should view your proposal or options as a logical conclusion to be drawn from the data provided. It is your professional approach to working toward a *winning* result for all parties that will set you apart from the competition.

Keep in mind that the process can take time; some deals may take months or even years. Stay in touch with prospects, because people who will not sell or buy now may do so later. I have bought houses that I first looked at several years before. It took that long for the sellers to come around, or perhaps conditions changed.

"Weasel" Clauses: The Key to Reducing Risk

Every contract should contain a "weasel," or contingency, clause that lets you legally back out of a contract should you decide not to go through with the purchase of a property. The weasel clause protects you during the controlling period so you can sleep at night.

After you negotiate the best price and the best terms possible, you *absolutely* must insert a contingency clause into the contract. Select from one of the following clauses, all of which I have used in contracts:

- Closing contingent on buyer's inspection and approval of condition of property before closing. (What if a storm hits the house or vandals break out every window? You should have a right to inspect the premises before closing!)

- Closing contingent on buyer obtaining favorable financing.
- Closing contingent on buyer's inspection and approval of utilities before closing.
- Closing contingent on buyer's partner's, spouse's, uncle's (whomever's) approval.
- Closing contingent on buyer's contractor's inspection and approval.
- Closing contingent on buyer obtaining a home inspection report agreeable to buyer.
- Closing contingent on contractor coming in and giving favorable bids to do the repairs (if it's a fixer-upper).
- Closing contingent on buyer's inspection and approval of all paperwork, leases, tenant histories, completed title work, etc.

Remember, closing can be contingent on anything you can think of if the seller allows you to insert it into the contract!

Weasel clauses essentially offer you a risk-free way to buy properties by giving you a way to back out of any purchase agreement. If you don't have a weasel clause, then you are bound by the contract and always must close. While I recommend that you never put a contract on a property that you don't fully intend to close on, just in case, you always should insert a weasel clause to give you a way out if your due diligence and research reveal a problem. Never enter into a contract for the purchase of real estate without a weasel clause. I don't do it; neither should you. If a seller will not let you put one into a contract, walk away—unless the deal is an absolute steal and you are 100 percent sure that you can and will buy it.

 R O B E R T ' S   R U L E S

If you have a motivated seller, you should be able to get the weasel (contingency) clauses you want.

More Important Points about Contracts

Contracts are written from the point of view of either the buyer or the seller. Very often, the seller of the real estate will want to provide his or her own contract. Do not let this bother you. I often do many things to make the seller feel as comfortable as possible. Then I can get the best deal possible. If the sellers insist on using their contract, go ahead and use it, but modify it to best suit your purposes.

Besides including your very low purchase price and favorable terms, your contract needs to spell out how you are going to take title to the property. How you take title to a property can greatly affect your liability and the transferability of the contract. It also may have grave implications for taxation down the road.

 R O B E R T ' S   R U L E S

Consult with a qualified attorney about drawing up and reviewing all of your real estate contracts, assignments, and paperwork.

Whenever I sign a contract or enter into a contract for the sale of real estate, I always insert "Robert Shemin or assigns." In nearly all states, contracts of almost any sort are assignable. That is, if you have a contract for the purchase of a house, a truckload of beans, or just about anything, you can transfer the *right* to buy it to someone else. Therefore, to ensure your right of assignability, you should put *"your name or assigns"* on each contract. That will legally give you the right to assign the contract to another buyer before the close in order to flip the property.

If uneasy sellers ask why you are putting "or assigns" in the contract, tell them that you may want to transfer the contract to another legal entity such as a trust, corporation, or partnership, or just another named party for the purpose of protecting your liability. Explain that most real estate contracts are assignable anyway.

Always have your contract reviewed by an attorney to make sure that it complies with your state's laws. You also may get a sample copy of a real estate contract from your local Board of Agents, a real estate agent, or an attorney. You can find an attorney referral network that can review your contracts by visiting my Web site, <www.shemin.com>.

Contracts are designed to protect both parties in a real estate deal. While it is very important for you to understand and trust the seller before you sign a contract, contracts can protect you from unscrupulous sellers. I work under the premise that hardly anyone can be trusted, so I put everything in a contract to protect myself.

Don't Allow Your Contract to Be Shopped

When you put a purchase agreement on a property, whether it's through an agent or the owner, never allow your contract to be "shopped." It is illegal for a real estate agent to do it and you can lose many good deals, too.

What is "shopping a contract?" Suppose you submit a purchase agreement on a property, and instead of accepting it, rejecting it, or making a counteroffer, the agent holds the contract and calls other potential buyers. Typically, the agent will ask other buyers, "I've got a contract on 100 Main Street for $30,000, can you offer more?"

To protect yourself from shopping, always insist on writing into the contract that the offer will expire and be voided in 24 hours, 2 days, 5 days, or in whatever time frame you choose. Make sure the sellers and/or their agent understand that you have other good deals and you cannot wait long for an answer. If you ever believe that an agent has shopped your contract, please report the agent to your local Board of Agents and/or to the agent's boss.

File Your Contract to Protect Your Claim

A contract alone may not be enough to protect you from unscrupulous sellers. A seller may sign a contract with you and then try to sell the property to someone else, leaving you out in the cold. To protect yourself after signing a contract, go to your local recording office (the office where documents regarding real estate are recorded) and file a letter or affidavit stating that you have a contract on the property, specifying the property address, the sellers' names, your name, and the purchase price. You also may need to submit a copy of the contract to be recorded and pay a transfer fee or tax for recording the affidavit.

Filing an affidavit will make it difficult if not impossible for the sellers to pass title or sell the property to someone else. Title cannot be passed because there is a public notice stating that you have a contract on that property. When a prospective title insurance company finds the copy of your contract or your affidavit stating that you have a contract on the property, it will not insure the title for the new purchasers.

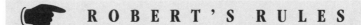

ROBERT'S RULES

To protect your claim, file an affidavit and a copy of the contract at the courthouse.

Recording your deals is much easier and more effective than suing. I discovered this very early on in my real estate career. I signed a contract with a seller who turned around and sold the property to another party, which was both unethical and illegal. On hearing of the sale, I raced down to the courthouse and filed an affidavit at my local recording office. I then called the new purchaser of the property and the sellers and told them that they could not do this to me. They laughed and said "Yes, we can, and there is nothing you can do about it." I then informed them that I had an affidavit and the contract filed at the courthouse before they had recorded their documents, and that they could never get title insurance or ever pass clear title to the property. They quit laughing and began negotiating. Because I was now in control, I negotiated a very fair settlement with them, but I didn't release my claim on the property until their check was cashed.

How to Hold a Property

With a contract in hand, you control a property. Once you close, take title, and transfer ownership to yourself or to your business, you hold the property, unless you flip or sell it immediately.

How you hold your property depends on how you organize your real estate business. There are four alternatives for organizing a business:

1. A *sole proprietorship,* meaning the business and everything associated with it is in your name
2. A *corporation,* whether a C corporation or a smaller type S corporation, meaning that the taxation is treated more like a partnership and the tax benefits and liabilities flow directly to you
3. A *partnership,* if you are going into business with someone else
4. A *limited liability company,* which can be great for running a real estate business

You also can set up a trust and hold the real estate in the trust's name, or you can form a limited partnership.

Each one of these influences how you take title to and hold a property. Let's look at these options individually.

 R O B E R T ' S   R U L E S

All titling decisions affect your income tax bracket, your liability for the property, and your estate taxes and planning—all complicated subjects best left to your accountants and attorneys. Your job is to find good deals, make money, and help people. Let the professionals help you select a titling strategy that best fits your situation.

Sole Proprietorship

In a sole proprietorship, you hold property in your own name or in your name and your spouse's name.

Corporations

In the eyes of the law, a corporation is a "person," so that your assets, property, and business now can be in a corporate name, not yours. Many people like to form corporations to appear more professional and you can give yourself a great title like president or chief executive officer.

If all of the papers, filings, and business dealings are done properly, a corporation will limit your liability. If an individual is sued, all of his or her assets are at risk. But if a corporation is sued, only what the corporation owns is at risk. However, all documents must be signed in the corporation name and must include your title, for example, president. You also must follow all incorporation procedures, be adequately insured, and maintain proper records and meetings. Many people set up corporations but do not keep adequate records and files, which can nullify a corporation.

SOLE PROPRIETORSHIP

Advantages: It's simple. Banks like it. Taxes are simple. Property is easy to transfer. You can put it in your will.

Disadvantages: You are an easy lawsuit target. Your name is on all public records. Should you be sued for anything, the assets in your name can and will be easily attached.

You can have investors in the corporation, and sell shares in the corporation instead of selling off the entire property. If a corporation owns ten houses, then you can sell off 10 percent of the corporation to raise money, instead of selling off one house, or one-tenth of your houses.

If you are going to be a landlord, you'll want to set up a property management corporation. The job of the property management company is to collect all rents, pay all bills, hire help, manage property, and procure insurance. Generally, the corporation charges the owners of the property a commission, anywhere from 8 to 25 percent of the gross rent. If your property management company is managing properties that you own, 10 percent is a good commission. This commission pays your salary and, with a corporation, you must take a salary. Remember, owning property and managing it are two different things.

When you set up a property management company, tenants will not know that you are the owner of the corporation or the owner of the properties. You can be the good guy, working for a mean owner. Tenants do not call you at home, because they do not know who the owner of the property is. A corporation is another layer of protection for you. It also makes you treat your business like a business: You work more regular hours, and it is separated from your personal life.

CORPORATIONS

Advantages: Property is not in your name. With an S corporation, tax advantages such as depreciation pass directly to owner. A big protection from personal liability, you easily can give away and sell property.

Disadvantages: Cumbersome taxes and paperwork that must be done properly. Banks will loan money to corporations, but may require a personal guarantee. Also, the corporation must be separately insured, and the corporate veil can be "pierced" to get to you.

General Partnership

Anytime two or more people either officially (in writing) or by their actions decide who runs a business, they are probably deemed to be general partners. That is, everyone in the partnership is involved in the decision making and management of the partnership. If there is nothing in writing, but you and your "partner" act like partners, you might have a general partnership. You probably never want to be a general partner, because you are typically liable for everything—including your partner's actions.

GENERAL PARTNERSHIP

Advantages: Simple to set up. Allows you to partner deals immediately.

Disadvantages: All partners generally are liable for the actions of the other partners, which is not a good way to own real estate.

Limited Partnership

A limited partnership (LP) is made up of a general partner and one or more limited partners. The general partner controls and runs the partnership; the limited partners cannot participate in decision making or management of the L.P. or the property it holds. While the general partner is typically liable for all of the partners' actions, the limited partner only can lose what limited investments or contributions he or she put into the LP. Limited partnership papers must be filed and the L.P. will issue annual tax statements to the partners. Many large real estate investments are held this way.

Limited Liability Company

A limited liability company (LLC) is a new type of corporation that combines all the advantages and flexibility of partnerships and corporations, and also limits your liability. I recommend looking into forming an LLC and most attorneys and accountants seem to agree that it is probably the best way to own real estate. You can have a one-person LLC in many states, and even though your liability is limited to what is in the LLC, you can participate in management. You can decide whether you would like to be taxed as an individual, a partnership, or a corporation. Of course, as with all forms of corporations, you must file the proper documents with the state, as well as file the appropriate tax documents.

LIMITED PARTNERSHIPS

Advantages: Great asset protection, except for the general partner, who should be a corporation, and will be held liable. It also is a good estate planning tool, as limited partnership interests can get a discount because they are not easily marketed as real estate owned outright.

Disadvantages: The general partner is liable, and there are some complex tax compliance issues that entail paperwork. There also are costs involved in setting up an LP.

Land Trusts

Trusts are a popular option for many investors. There are many different types, including living trusts (which are sometimes used instead of wills), revocable trusts (which can be changed at any time), and irrevocable trusts (which cannot be changed). There is also a special type of trust for real estate, commonly referred to as a *land trust.*

The general principle of a trust is simple: By creating a trust, you are entrusting another person (or other legal entity) with an asset or piece of property. The person who manages the trust is called the trustee and probably has the highest legal duty known in law. That high legal duty is to the beneficiary of the trust, who could be yourself, your children, or whomever receives the benefits of what the trust owns. The trustee's duty is a fiduciary one; that is, the trustee must do whatever the trust tells him or her to do and also must do what is in the best interest of the beneficiaries of that trust.

The main benefit of using a land trust is that the real estate is not in your name. I cannot think of one benefit of having property in your name—unless, of course, you want to impress someone with how much property you own. In just a few minutes, I could go to the office where documents regarding real estate are recorded and look up your property address and find your name and/or your spouse's name. I also easily could call the property tax assessor's office and obtain the same information over the phone. Most states now have computerized systems so that, in a matter of seconds, I can discover all of the property that you own in any given county.

LIMITED LIABILITY COMPANY

Advantages: Offers the same protection as a corporation, but with more flexibility, along with flexible tax advantages. Available in almost all states now.

Disadvantages: It's very new and most states only recently have enacted LLC statutes. The IRS or some creative lawyer may find loopholes to attach liability to you.

Unfortunately, the people who are most likely to look into how property is titled or to determine what assets are in your name are attorneys who are attempting to sue you. If you're being sued, an attorney can go to the courthouse, punch up your name, and find all the property you own. If you have substantial assets or own some real estate, it will show that you are a great person to sue because you have funds.

A land trust protects you from frivolous lawsuits and litigation by setting up a road block that most litigants will have trouble knocking down. When a property is taken in the name of a land trust, it is no longer in your name; it is now in the name of the trust. You can give whatever name you want to the trust (for example, if you buy 100 Apple Street, you could call it the 100 Apple Street Trust) and should set up a separate trust for each property you buy. Therefore, if you own a lot of property and someone looks up addresses, all they will find are the names of the trusts and the names of the trustees. You can name anyone as trustees—friends, relatives, accountants, or attorneys—as long as they are legal, competent adults. When a researcher calls the trustee and asks, "Hey, Mr. or Mrs. Trustee, who owns 100 Apple Street (or who is the beneficiary of this trust)?" the trustee will be instructed to say, "I am sorry, as trustee I cannot tell you." A good lawyer will then ask, "Where can I find a copy of the trust so I can look up and see who the beneficiary is?" The trustee's response is simple: "Well, it is locked in my safe and I am not permitted to show it to you."

The only way for someone to find out who owns the property is to obtain a court order for the trustee to divulge the trust or reveal the name of the beneficiary, which is a major hassle, to say the least. Keep in mind that a property can be traced to you if you transfer a property into a trust after it has already been in your name—although it will require some tedious research on the part of attorneys, and some confine their efforts to calling up the tax assessor's office or taking a quick trip down to where deeds are recorded to see what comes up in your name. That's why although land trusts cannot absolutely guarantee privacy and protection, they do ensure that it will take litigants longer to find out what you own.

Let's look at another scenario: Suppose a litigant discovers (by word of mouth) that you are the owner of a certain piece of property on which his or her lawyer believes a claim can be made. If you are dragged into court and asked on the witness stand, "Do you own any property?" you can legally answer, "No." Why? Because the trust owns the property; you are only the beneficiary of the trust. A smart lawyer will ask, however, "Are you the beneficiary of any assets or do you have a beneficial interest in any property?" Then, of course, you must answer yes. An Atlanta, Georgia, real estate developer in big trouble with banks was able to keep his real estate held in trust because during a deposition the bank's lawyers—some of the best attorneys in Atlanta—asked him, "Do you own any other real estate?" The real estate developer said, "No." They also asked, "Do you own any other property or assets?" and again he answered, "No." When the developer was discharged from the case, he was able to keep many millions of dollars' worth of real estate. The banks would have gotten back most or all of the property had the lawyers only asked, "Are you the beneficial owner of any interests in real estate," or "Do you have any other interests in real estate?"

Land trusts also provide you with anonymity when you buy and sell properties. Many real estate investors do not like having the whole world know what they own, buy, and sell. Large companies like Wal-Mart or K-mart use land trusts to purchase property to keep the cost of land from escalating when a seller discovers that a Fortune 500 company wants to buy it.

Anonymity can be a great benefit for smaller investors when they buy and sell real estate.

I also buy, own, and sell in a trust. Many times when I flip a property, I don't want the end buyer or seller to know how much I'm making. When a property is held in trust, my name is not on the property, the trustee's is. The trustee signs all the documents, receives all the notices on the property, and handles all matters concerning the property for me. My name is never mentioned, so no one knows how much I made on the deal. Also, because the property was never in my name, I never had any direct liability.

Trusts also have disadvantages. Trusts mean paperwork, and finding a trustee to handle all transactions regarding the real estate may cost some money. Also, having property titled in a trust may confuse lenders, who still want you to personally guarantee the property because it is not really in your name. Many people and banks wrongly believe that transferring property into a trust will trigger the due-on-sale clause in your mortgage. Not true. Federal banking law confirms that a transfer of a property into a trust does not trigger the due-on-sale clause. Nevertheless, it may be a point of confusion for unsophisticated lenders and cause borrowing delays.

LAND TRUSTS

Advantages: Make it difficult, but not impossible, to determine the owner of the property. The trustee does not have to tell anyone who owns the property unless a court orders it revealed. If you sell or flip the property, no one has to know you are involved or are making money. Should you be sued, it will take the attorney a long time to find out you own the property, or he or she may never find out.

Disadvantages: Trustee has to sign all documents—and you must trust the trustee. Also, banks get a little confused and a land trust offers no real asset protection; top attorneys can break through them. There are no tax or estate differences.

There are no income tax implications for having property titled in the name of a land trust and it really does not affect the way you file your tax returns, except that you may have to list that the property is held in a trust.

How to Protect a Property

Every property must be protected with title insurance, liability insurance, and property and casualty insurance.

Don't believe me? I know someone who bought 50 acres of land in a little town outside Nashville for about $100,000—dirt cheap in that neck of the woods. Because the previous owners had owned the property for many years, he figured there would be no problems with title. To save a couple hundred dollars at the closing, he opted not to buy title insurance.

A few years later, a major car company built a factory right next to that land and its value skyrocketed into the millions. That's when the railroad decided to reclaim the land, which had a railroad lien on the property dating from 1910. My friend saved $200 and lost millions. If he had purchased title insurance, the title company would have discovered the lien and cleared up the problem.

Another acquaintance bought a house to fix up on the weekends. Because the property was vacant, he decided to save $500 and postpone purchasing property and casualty insurance. He rued his decision the weekend the house burned to the ground and he was out $60,000.

Don't be penny wise and pound foolish. Take every measure you can to properly protect your property!

Title Insurance

Title insurance is exactly what it sounds like: It insures title by guaranteeing on purchase that you have good and clear title. Title insurance companies, such as Chicago Title or Stewart Title, are insurance companies that insure property title. You absolutely must get title insurance whenever you buy property!

Usually sellers pay for title insurance; that is, they insure that the title they give you is good. The title company will do their own title

ROBERT'S RULES

You can use land trusts to title some of your properties. I like to use them when I flip or lease-option a property. When filling out a contract, it keeps things out of your name. If you plan to buy a lot of real estate, you probably want to contact local counsel about forming a limited liability company if it is available in your state. S corporations and limited partnerships also can be very beneficial for purchasing and holding real estate. Consult your attorney and your accountant to find out which form of ownership is best for your personal circumstances.

search or have their lawyers do a title search—informing you of the chain of title, who owns it, and what, if any, liens exist, such as a mortgage, property taxes, and any judgments. This is especially important for distressed properties. Normally when you buy a property for cash or borrow the money to buy it, the money is used to pay off all of the debt and liens against the property. But if there are other liens or problems, the title company will attempt to resolve them before issuing a title insurance policy. If the title cannot be cleared, you will not be able to get title insurance—but then you shouldn't buy the property, either!

At every closing, make sure to read and understand this title insurance policy, as it may have exceptions in the back. Most of the time these exceptions are what are called utility easements; that is, easements allowing utility companies to run lines or water pipes or sewers across your property. These should be no problem for you, as you shouldn't mind having these utilities available to your house. However, make sure you understand all the exceptions on your title policy.

If for any reason there is ever a problem with the title, the title company will defend you in any actions concerning this title. Therefore, just as with most types of insurance, if you have title insurance, you don't have to worry about the quality of your title, as long as you understand any exceptions in that policy.

Title insurance costs vary from state to state. Before buying any property, make sure that the closing agent, attorney, or title company explains all of the closing costs and title insurance to you. Ask other real estate investors, banks, or mortgage companies to recommend a good title company, and try to do all of your closings or purchasing and selling there so that you have a good resource for any title questions that may come up.

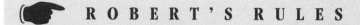

ROBERT'S RULES

Never buy property without title insurance. You always want to know that there is a clear title to the property that you are buying.

Liability and Property and Casualty Insurance

Every property you have title to must be insured against damage, loss, or potential liability.

Ask other investors, real estate agents, and people at your real estate association for the name of a good real estate insurance broker. Tell the broker exactly what you will be doing—buying, renting, fixing, and selling properties—and ask him or her to recommend the proper insurance and the right amount of it. All recommendations should be put in writing and kept as future protection should you find that you did not have enough insurance. Your insurance and the insurance on the people who work on your properties are your most important protection. Make sure you have it.

Vacant property often is difficult and expensive to insure. Shop around, but make sure you are insured for the full *replacement value* of the property. If you rehab the property and hold on to it for many years, make sure your policy adjusts for inflation. You should review your policies annually. If you don't, you could be underinsured in a few years. For rental property, you can insure appliances for just a few dollars more a year; of course, if your deductible is high, it does not pay to insure them. Remember, anything attached to the property, such as central heating and air or hot water heaters, usually is insured under your general policy.

Everyone who works on your properties should have worker's compensation insurance. What would happen if someone working on your property fell off a ladder and was injured? Whether the person broke a foot or their neck, many state courts would hold you liable for those injuries. Ask for proof of worker's compensation insurance. If someone working on your property doesn't have worker's compensation, deduct the premium out of their pay and buy it for them. The cost is based on dollars earned and type of work. It is the only way to avoid costly liability in the event that an uninsured worker gets hurt on one of your properties.

Whenever you use people to work on your properties, also make sure they are subcontractors, not employees. If workers are hurt and they are not insured, courts typically will find you liable. The best protection is to have workers sign subcontractor agreements and check with local counsel. Generally, your regular insurance will not cover workers hurt on your jobs. If they are subcontractors, they should be responsible for their own actions, injuries, and insurance. Each state varies, but some general rules about people working on your properties are to make sure that they

- use their own tools;
- either work for others (and not you), set their own hours, do not clock in, or they are their own bosses;
- have their own transportation and insurance, and their own policies and procedures (for employees); and
- carry their own worker's compensation insurance.

Subcontractors who work for you a majority of their time may be considered your employees by the government. In this situation, a rehabber may be considered a general contractor. The contracting business will be regarded as separate from your primary business and may not be covered by your existing insurance. You also may need to purchase general contractor's insurance—even if you don't think of yourself as a general contractor! This is a mistake that many rehabbers make. Check with your attorney to see if you are at risk of being considered a general contractor.

It is important to make sure that any property you have title to is properly insured. Sometimes investment property can be added to your current homeowners policy. If possible, purchase a large umbrella policy that will cover your cars, personal property, and up to five rental properties.

Meet with your insurance agent annually to see if you are adequately insured. Shop around for the best policies and prices. Once you get more than a few policies you may be able to put them all under one policy, commonly referred to as a blanket policy. Blanket policies of $1,000,000 or more of protection usually are only $500 to $1,000 a year above the total costs of your normal policies.

Assess your risks, the types of judgments assessed in your state, and how much and what type of insurance you have. If you have a lot of risk and a lot of assets, you probably need a lot of insurance. Buying extra insurance may be more effective and much simpler than forming and maintaining complex corporations or partnerships. Adequate insurance is probably the best and the simplest protection you can get!

 R O B E R T ' S   R U L E S

Overinsure yourself. Talk to your attorney and insurance agent about all of these liabilities and protect yourself!

Insurance Coverage Checklist

Go over this checklist with your insurance agent.

❏ Are you the insured named on every property that you own or have an interest in? Never buy or close on a property without having your name on an insurance policy that protects you and the property.

❏ Do you have all the insurance in place that your agent recommended? If you are repairing properties, do you need worker's compensation insurance or contractors'- or builders'-risk insurance?

❏ How much insurance do you need—$300,000, $500,000, $1 million, $2 million, or more? Your insurance agent will know.

❏ If you own a property in a trust or corporation, is that entity named as an insured? If a corporation or trust owns a property, then it must be named on the policy.

❏ Do your workers and contractors have proof of insurance? Don't take their word for it. Get a copy of a valid insurance policy.

❏ Do you have *replacement value insurance* on your property (insurance that, in essence, keeps up with the value of the property)? If your property appreciates over time and you do not have replacement insurance, you may get less than what the property is worth.

CHAPTER 6

How to Sell a Property

It's a funny thing about life, if you refuse to accept anything but the best, you very often get it.

—W. Somerset Maugham

You've purchased a good deal, and you're ready to sell. Now what? If you don't want to buy, fixup, and hold a property as a landlord, there are three ways to sell a property:

1. You can wholesale the property to other investors (a type of equity flipping).
2. You can fix it up, either through your own sweat equity or through hiring contractors, and sell it retail to a prospective homebuyer.
3. You can fix it up and sell it to a nonprofit organization that will use it to house needy people.

If you are selling to other investors, you can contact your list of investment buyers or look in the newspaper for people who buy property. If you are selling to homebuyers, you may want to use a real estate agent. While many people say it does not pay to use a real estate agent to sell your property, I find that using a good agent can save a lot of time, which frees you up to find more good deals. Agents work hard for their commissions. Besides, if you bought the property at a 20 to 30 percent discount, then you certainly can afford to pay an agent a commission of 3 to 7 percent of the sales price. Look for an agent who is particularly active and successful in the area in which the property is located. I look for For Sale signs or read the newspaper to see who is listing a lot of houses for sale in that area.

Many nonprofit organizations that provide low-income houses and dwellings are buyers and long-term renters of residential properties. I have sold dozens of properties to nonprofit organizations, which have used them for housing groups such as runaway teenagers, recovering alcoholics, and the mentally challenged. You'll make money and help people by contacting your local United Way, city and state housing authority, Catholic Charities, and other nonprofits or charity groups that house people. These groups can help you determine whether zoning laws in your area will permit a group home.

No matter whether you want to sell your building wholesale, retail, or to a nonprofit organization, you need to begin by preparing the building for sale.

Preparing a Property for Sale

To sell a property, you need to prepare it properly in order to secure a price close to actual market value. Often the asking price is a matter of what appeals emotionally to prospective buyers. A National Association of REALTORS® study concluded that most buyers decide emotionally within the first two minutes whether they are seriously interested in a house. Many make their decision as soon as they enter the front door. Further, a University of California, Los Angeles, communications researcher noted that your visual message counts the most when people decide whether or not to believe you.

In other words, it's how things *look* that count. That's why you need to dress up your properties, concentrating your efforts on both the exterior and the entryway of the house.

I begin preparing a property by conducting little focus groups with people in the neighborhood and people who care to look at the property. I ask them what they like and what they don't like. Most of the time they are happy to tell me what colors they like and what they would want and not want. While friends and your significant other also can contribute their two cents, talking to neighbors may sell a house for you. Neighbors know people who might be interested and will talk to people who look at your house. Another way to find out what is "in" is to consult with new home builders whose business is to keep up with these things. Real estate agents are also very knowledgeable.

The high-perceived value items I've found that are particularly helpful in selling a home include:

- Ceiling fans
- Brass kick plates
- Brass address plates
- Well-tended landscaping
- Flowers in the house
- Miniblinds
- New toilet seats
- Used appliances that look new
- Alarm system
- Neutral carpeting and colors
- Flowers and bushes in the front yard
- Brass lamps by the front door

These items are not expensive and they will make a property emotionally more appealing. They will enhance the property's desirability and can make your offer more enticing. What's more, it will dramatically show that the property has been properly maintained. Adding these components also will encourage agents to show your property, should you decide to go that route.

"To-Do" Checklist to Prepare a Property for Sale

Exterior

❏ Landscaping should look presentable.

❏ Trim all trees and shrubs.

❏ Rake leaves, mow and edge lawn.

❏ Edge driveway.

❏ Install shutters.

❏ Install large house numbers on front of home.

❏ Install decorative front door (or repaint).

❏ Paint using semigloss (paint front first).

❏ Install new windows, if needed (in front first).

Kitchen

❏ Be certain sink is clean and looks presentable.

❏ Install cabinet fronts with new knobs.

❏ Install wallpaper with adequate borders.

❏ Hang or place a deodorizer.

❏ Install bright new linoleum on floor.

❏ Install decorative wall plugs.

❏ Install ceiling fans and miniblinds.

❏ Install working smoke/fire alarms and carbon monoxide detector.

❏ Cleanup appliances. (Appliances are not mandatory but add value.)

Bedrooms and Bathrooms

❏ Paint trim in semigloss with different colors.

❏ Refinish tub/shower and sink, if necessary.

❏ Consider putting cedar in all closets.

❏ Install neutral wallpaper with borders or paint.

❏ Install a ceiling fan (use light fixture, if applicable).

❏ Marolite over damaged walls, if necessary.

❏ Don't strip wood or restain.

❏ Replace outdated faucets.

❏ Install miniblinds.

❏ Put up new shower curtain.

❑ Install new carpet and pad, if necessary.

❑ Clean toilets using denture tablets or similar product.

Living Room

❑ Install molding at ceiling.

❑ Use some decorative paneling, if appropriate.

❑ Install new carpet and padding.

❑ Install inexpensive curtains or miniblinds.

❑ Install ceiling fans (use light fixture, if applicable).

Don't Overspend!

Overspending on renovation gets many sellers into deep water. In an effort to glamorize a property, they go overboard and spend far too much, thinking it will increase the property value and make it easier to sell. They want everything to be perfect, immaculate, and to their taste. They overlook the fact that prospects don't necessarily want to live in a house that matches the sellers' own taste. Everyone is looking for something different. Don't try to second-guess by adding unnecessary touches! My prospects in the low- and middle-income neighborhoods are looking for nice, clean, fresh places, not palaces.

While you *do* want to give your property a higher than normal market value, you don't need to overspend to do so. Bathrooms and kitchens do sell a property, but you needn't spend a fortune on cabinets or vanities. It's far better to maximize your profit by concentrating on basic, clean items that work. Keep the amenities fairly nice, neat, and clean and the colors neutral so the new occupants can come in and put their finishing (and personal) touches on it.

Ask around to find out what buyers in your area want. For example, in one of my communities, people like decks attached to their home. By spending an extra $800 to put a deck on a home, I get a lot more money for the property.

Are central air and heat necessary in the community? If so, you can buy a slightly used system. I also use basic and inexpensive carpets for flooring. I also install inexpensive miniblinds or window shades to make a place look nice—people love them. It's a can't-miss way to tempt prospects into making a positive decision. As a matter of fact, I put in miniblinds or window shades whenever I buy a property, whether I'm going to sell it or rent it, because they also prevent lookers from peeking in the windows.

Modest landscaping, some bushes and flowers, is not expensive and will increase the value of a home by 5 to 10 percent. If you're short of cash on a particular deal and you believe it's necessary to get the land-scaping in better shape to get top dollar, you may be able to get the job done without using your own money. Approach a landscaper and say, "Look, if you do the landscaping on this job and you'll wait two months (or whatever time it takes) for your money until I sell the home, I'll pay you double your ordinary fee." If you can get one landscaper to go for this deal, you can save a great deal of up-front money. You also can try this gambit with appliance, carpeting, paint, plumbing, drapery, and other individual contractors as well.

Do whatever it will take to sell the property, but don't go crazy. The point is, you have to determine what it will take to motivate some-one to buy your property without putting you in a bind. Remember, every dollar you spend can increase the price of the property, perhaps even above normal market value.

Finding and Working with Contractors

Whether you rehab buildings to sell or repair properties to rent, you need to work with responsible contractors and handymen who will do a first-rate job for a fair price. No simple task! Remember, there are an awful lot of bad apples in the container. If you're not involved and watching closely, you're going to be sorry.

Many unscrupulous contractors will make the work sound simple, and their price will sound fair. But, sure enough, they'll end up drinking on the job, killing time, overcharging, failing to show up, doing shoddy work, or working on another job that takes precedent because they sud-denly received cash up front from some unwary client. And you're stuck.

The best way to find good contractors is to ask for referrals from people you know—other investors, members of your real estate associa-tion, real estate agents or brokers, or property management companies. The managers of the major home improvement stores also may be able to refer someone good.

ROBERT'S RULES

Determining a property's selling price depends on your knowledge of what the market will bear. Factors such as the retail price of other houses in the area (pull up three to eight comparable sales, either online or from an agent), how much work needs to be done on the house, and what investors typically pay for houses in that area, will aid you in your decision.

Ask contractors for references, and check them. Make sure the contractors you use are licensed, bonded, and insured. Worker's compensation is the national and state system that provides for workers who get hurt on the job. An uninsured contractor could cost you a lot of your hard-earned money. Just imagine what could happen to your assets if an uninsured worker falls off a roof. Consult your insurance agent and attorney concerning liability when you're dealing with contractors, and make it a point to get proof of insurance! If a contractor does not have it, it's wise to deduct the premiums from the money you're going to pay for the project and purchase the workers' compensation insurance for him.

Quite honestly, I've used people who were not licensed and bonded, and occasionally gotten far better prices—but there is a lot of risk involved. I like to search for people who moonlight, such as roofers who work on weekends to make ends meet. Some real estate people I know approach workmen they see while driving around and ask if they're interested in working on one of their properties on their time off or on weekends. However, by using people who are not licensed and bonded, you may lose your money if something goes wrong—and you may face enormous liability if someone uninsured is hurt on the job.

I believe it's better to get the best even if it costs a few extra dollars. If you skimp by using a substandard contractor, you may regret it. More than once I've saved $100 only to spend $1,000 to repair a problem when a substandard contractor didn't do the work right. Until you know contractors well, stick to professionals. You can be sure their work will meet all codes and regulations.

Once you find good contractors, treat them fairly. If they are writing up a lot of bids for you but you are not using them, pay them a fee.

Give them a bonus if they do a good job and finish on time. Refer them for other jobs. Treat them to a nice dinner. Cultivate a long-term working relationship by working with the same responsible people. If you patronize the same heat and air-conditioning person, the same appliance man, the same painter, and so on, you get good dependability and prices (although I do "shop" them from time to time in order to keep them honest).

To protect yourself, never pay a contractor by the hour. *Never.* I've found that if you pay by the hour, all of a sudden a 15-hour paint job takes 50 hours. Instead, pay by the job. Other measures you can take to protect yourself include the following:

- Get three competitive written bids.
- Monitor the work continuously.
- Never become dependent on one contractor (let them all know that!).
- Provide very low draws—just enough to cover costs of materials.
- Don't pay until the work is 100 percent complete, and hold back a substantial portion of payment until after you have inspected it to make sure it is acceptable.

If work is incomplete beyond a set date, charge the contractor a penalty. Time is money. If your property is not ready, then it costs you. I levy a $50 a day penalty because I want my contractors to understand that cost savings and quality work permeate every nook and cranny of my company. No exceptions! I let them know in advance that every day they are not done on time costs me money, either in lost rent or depressed profits. And I don't intend to suffer their irresponsibility alone. In these competitive times, few companies can afford to take even a single contractor for granted and assume they will meet their obligations.

If you use part-time workers as independent subcontractors you should:

- make them responsible for their own insurance and tax requirements.
- put a clause in their contract stating that independent workers shall not hold you or your company liable for any claims arising from any cause on any job. The liability for each job is the sole responsibility of the bidder alone.

Make sure you inspect the following areas and that they are cleared by the appropriate utility:

- Electrical after final inspector check
- Roof after a significant rainfall
- Heating, ventilating, and air-conditioning after five days of continuous operation
- Plumbing after inspecting supply and drainpipes and fixtures
- Trash/hauling after dump receipts and invoices provided

I tell contractors that all bids, without exception, must include the following:

- Start date
- Estimate of time to complete and finish job. Job must be completed on time and in a quality manner. Substandard materials will not be permitted. Disputes over substandard work will be arbitrated by a codes inspector.
- If damage occurs during performance of a job, repairs will be deducted from the bid price.

My contracts specify that drugs or alcohol of any kind on the job is cause for instant termination. Smoking is not permitted on the job and must take place outside the job area.

I also like to get complete background information on everyone who works on one of my properties. I rely on large, licensed, and bonded contractors to have that information on file, but for smaller companies or independent contractors, I ask each worker to submit the following information before I accept their bid:

- Name
- Driver's license number
- Date of birth
- Social Security number
- Make and model of car or truck, and license number
- Work and home phone numbers
- Present address
- Three references less than a year old
- Proof of workers' compensation insurance

Identifying and Attracting Potential Buyers

By now you've compiled a network of private investors who are interested in purchasing the type of property you're selling. You also may consider adding some nonprofit organizations to your network list. Yours may be just the type of business opportunity some of these people may want to be let in on.

Your network is the first place to look for buyers. Letters to your list will be extremely effective, especially letters addressed to members of local real estate investment clubs. I send out the following letter as soon as I have an option on a house:

Right of First Refusal

Dear Valued Club Member,

As a courtesy to members of the Real Estate Club, I am sending you this advance notification of my intent to sell an exceptional piece of property that I have recently rehabbed.

I am extending the Right of First Refusal to those of you who might have an interest in advance of knowledge to any other investors.

If you want to avail yourself of this quite remarkable investment opportunity, I suggest you contact me rather quickly at 000-0000.

I am extending this Right of First Refusal to you because I believe (from previous conversations with several club members) that the property is essentially what you are seeking.

On the next page is a description of the property. If you have a serious interest, please call my secretary to schedule a meeting.

Sincerely,

Your Name

P.S. I've seen it time after time. Some will take a "wait and see" approach, while some will act now and make money while others are sitting and watching from the sidelines.

To find buyers who are not already on your list, use the following techniques. Most people rely on just one or two. You should use them all!

- Look in your local newspaper.
- Take out an ad in the newspaper.
- Check with real estate agents.
- Check with nonprofit organizations who sponsor group homes.
- Send a mailing to real estate clubs.
- Check with prospects you've met at auctions.
- Use signs and fliers.

To attract a prospect's attention, I use headlines on letters, ads, fly-ers, and all other communications that promise a benefit. Then I measure the results.

The headline's job is to target the prospect, get the prospect to read the rest of the copy, and, finally, to get the prospect to act by sending in a coupon, making a phone call, or responding to a call to action.

A good headline hits a prospect like lightning and promises a big, believable benefit fast. It offers an immediate solution so the reader is prompted to act! In a way, a good headline bends the will of the person who reads it or listens to it. Somehow it has the right words strung together and hits the reader's hot button (one of his or her needs or desires), and appeals to the reader's emotions. The headline that makes it happen is the heart and soul of direct response advertising.

Here are some headlines that have worked for me:

- Local real estate owner swears under oath he did not steal house he's selling so cheaply.
- Would you like a low-risk investment that can bring you a 20% annualized return?
- Foreclosure for sale. Comparable houses on block going for $15,000 more.

Each of these headlines offers prospective buyers a way to save or make money. Try to identify and offer the precise benefit buyers are looking for, so you will stir up a prospect's interest and get him or her to act.

The Postcard Strategy

One strategy that you can use to bring in more investors than you can hope to handle is a simple postcard mailing. All you need is your network list of potential buyers, a supply of inexpensive postcards, and an answering machine that will let you record a message at least two minutes in length. Run some postcards through your printer with the following message:

Dear Friend,

Would you like to learn about a house that I have for sale, at below market value, that's truly an exceptional bargain? Fact is, it seems incredible that I can offer this house for this price.

If you would like to learn more, all you have to do is call 000-0000 to hear a FREE recorded message. It will reveal probably the best piece of real estate to be offered in a long time.

Sincerely,

Your Name

Send a postcard to everybody on your list. I have found that pink or brightly colored postcards get the recipient's attention fast.

Next, prepare a little telephone script. It might read like this:

Thank you for calling. My name is _____ . I've been involved in the community here for ten years and I'm proud to say I know many of my neighbors personally. As a result, from time to time I find a wonderful piece of property with great potential, spend the necessary money to get it in really good condition, and then sell it for a modest profit. If you are interested, I'm sure we can work out the terms that fit your budget best. That's my job. I look forward to meeting you soon and talking to you about financing, points, and closing. Please call me at 000-0000 and tell me when you're available and we'll get together so you can see what a wonderful bargain I have in store for you. Of course, there is no obligation whatsoever.

Practice reading the script a few times and record it on your answering machine. Then mail your postcards and sit back and wait for the phone to ring off the hook. Why does this work so well? Because:

- It presents a bargain and perhaps financial security.
- It's totally nonthreatening to a prospect.
- It offers an easy way to get free information.
- The caller listens to a voice that sounds sincere, trustworthy, and caring.
- You offer a no-risk, no-obligation proposition.

Marketers know that people often have a stronger desire to avert loss than to gain a potential advantage. What people typically try to avoid is losing money or being ripped off, emotional pain, wasting time, and worry. The reason this marketing concept works is that you're dealing with basic human appeals. The trick is to experiment and discover what appeal is best for your particular business.

This technique can work no matter what kind of offer you want to make, including purchasing real estate or offering a property for sale by owner.

You also may want to try running a small postcard ad in your local newspaper. All it requires is a small change in the look of the copy. Here's an example:

Want to buy a house at below-market value that's truly an exceptional bargain? It seems incredible that I can offer this house for this price. Call 000-0000 to listen to a FREE recorded message. Call anytime, 24 hours a day.

Here are a few more ads that are sure to bring out highly motivated buyers in droves:

Divorce Forces Local Owner to Practically Give Away House. Call 000-0000 for an appointment anytime, 24 hours a day.

(You can substitute "banker" or "money problems" and so on for "divorce.")

Local Real Estate Owner Swears Under Oath He Did Not Steal House He's Selling So Cheaply. Call 000-0000 for an appointment. Call anytime, 24 hours a day.

THIS HOUSE IS A REAL STEAL. Call 000-0000 for an appointment. Call 24 hours a day.

FORECLOSURE FOR SALE. Comparable houses on block going for $15,000 more. Property is going for 25% less than others per square foot.

In all of my letters, ads, fliers, and phone messages, I let the prospect know that there is no risk in doing business with me. I talk benefits. I educate. I offer multiple options. I offer to do all the document work. I offer something free. I romance people by stressing my personal service. I create the impression that I'm the one at risk.

Follow Up on Prospects

Reply immediately to prospects who respond to your ads and direct mail. When possible (unless your ad specifies otherwise), handle all calls personally and within 24 hours.

When you reach the prospect, determine quickly what the caller is seeking. Be educational and avoid forceful sales techniques. Describe the property, and then ask questions to qualify the prospect. When you are satisfied that you are talking to a serious buyer, provide him or her with the property address. If the prospect is preapproved for a loan, arrange to show the property.

Of course, it's a given that you should record every prospect name, address, phone number, and job status for your mailing list—even names of people who aren't quite ready to buy but are definitely looking.

Open Houses

Open houses can be a very effective way to generate interest and excitement in a property.

Encouraging several prospects to arrive at the same time will show them that others are interested, which often will prompt an immediate decision. My experience has shown that it's also a good idea to let peo-

ROBERT'S RULES

The National Association of REALTORS® asserts that over 70 percent of all real estate sales come from signs. So get a good sign, or if you're using a real estate agent, make sure your agent has one. Also, make sure your agent is running a good ad to sell your property.

ple know that "this property is going to go quickly." Not to mention that a single showing will save you countless hours and plenty of gasoline.

Schedule your open house for one to two hours early on a Saturday or Sunday afternoon. Advertise it in the newspaper, and hand out flyers to up to 200 of the neighbors. To save time, have a student distribute the flyers into doors and under windshield wipers. Many neighbors have family or friends who might be interested in buying in that neighborhood.

Prepare an attractive fact sheet that addresses every possible question a potential buyer could ask. Include a picture of the property, its address, the sales price, and your name and phone number. Provide the dimensions of each room and describe any special features, such as historical charm, fireplace, a pool, and so on. List the school district and disclose typical annual taxes and utilities. (For examples, look at what top real estate agents prepare for their showings.)

When visitors arrive, give each one a fact sheet. Have some candy, baked goods, and a nice-smelling potpourri out to enhance people's impression of the home. Don't worry about nerves. When you show the property, chances are you'll do a better job than a real estate agent. Tell me: Who is in a better position to know it more thoroughly than you? Who is more interested in selling it? Who has thoroughly researched the area? The answer is: You. Be friendly. Be excited about the property you're offering for sale. Be polite. Be professional. Let the house sell itself.

Just remember: *Never* show a house until it's absolutely ready to be sold, and it's ready to be occupied!

Once You Find a Buyer

Once you attract a buyer, place yourself in the seat of your potential prospect. Have a dialog, not a monologue, with each individual. Never assume what the prospect needs or wants. Ask what he or she is looking for: What turns him or her on? What turns him or her off? You can only do this if you get out and look at the neighborhood, schools in the area, and playgrounds, and find out about crime in the surrounding district, available churches, etc. Try not to be defensive. That can be tough with some buyers.

 ROBERT'S RULES

Working with Real Estate Agents

Because I take a team approach to real estate investing, I like to use real estate agents to sell my houses. Follow these guidelines when selling a house with an agent:

- Deal with active agents and brokers who buy and sell a lot of homes in the area.

- Ask for a written plan showing how the agent plans to market, promote, and sell the house.

- Negotiate a discounted commission schedule in exchange for letting the agent list other properties for you and for referring buyers and sellers.

- Sign a 90-day listing agreement to encourage the agent to get busy selling your property right away. Don't tie up the property with an agent for six months or a year, or it will certainly take that long to sell!

- Include a buyout agreement so that if you sell the house on your own, you pay the agent a small commission or none at all.

Find out how serious the prospect is about buying a house, when he or she wants to buy, and why. You want to deal with someone who is ready to buy and not just kicking tires, which is often the case with many people who attend open houses.

Informal chats with prospects can be tough work, but it's the only way to help you avoid the biggest pitfall investors and agents make: selling the property backwards. That is, they find a buyer, spend a great deal of time negotiating, keep the property tied up for 30 days while they wait to see if their potential buyer's loan is approved, then—after all this time and effort—they discover the buyer's loan is not approved.

Don't make this mistake. When you talk to anyone seriously interested in buying your property, run a credit check first. You wouldn't loan someone, even a friend, $50,000 without first running a credit check, would you? Yet that's just what a number of sellers fail to do. If you don't run a check, the contents of that credit report could come back to haunt you. More than 50 percent of all real estate contracts fail because the buyer cannot get a loan! Check with a property manager in your area to find a reliable firm that does credit checks.

Also, make sure that your potential buyer is preapproved by a bank or a mortgage company before you spend time showing a house or negotiating a contract. This will help both you and the buyer avoid a lot of frustration and disappointment. If the buyer is not preapproved but has good credit, steer him or her to your favorite mortgage company or bank. Don't begin to negotiate until you know the buyer can get financing.

 R O B E R T ' S   R U L E S

Never sign a contract to sell a property to anyone—another investor or a retail buyer—who is not preapproved for a loan or who cannot show you they have the means of getting the money to buy your property. If they say they are preapproved for a loan, get a letter from their banker or mortgage company. If they say they have the cash, have them show you a bank statement. They shouldn't mind doing so if they are serious about buying the property. In other words, don't spend a great deal of time with people who really cannot pay you.

Offer Creative Financing Alternatives

When I advertise a property, I don't talk about how much it costs. I talk about the kind of terms I will offer. Financing is what really sells a house. Instead of running a ho-hum ad for a $72,000 home, print: "$500 down and easy financing is all it takes to move into this beautiful home," or "$500 down and $625 a month will make this home yours!" You'll get a lot more calls!

Work with your mortgage broker to offer creative financing alternatives that make the sale viable and profitable and set you apart from other investors. Here are some alternatives to consider offering to retail buyers:

- Paying all closing costs.
- Offering a lease-to-own option.
- Helping the buyer cover the down payment through special government or bank programs for low- and moderate-income buyers or first-time homebuyers. Such a program might make it possible for a buyer to purchase an $80,000 home with as little as $500 down. Stay in touch with local banks and mortgage companies to keep abreast of which programs are available.
- Offering a special rebate. If it's legal and ethical in your area, offer a $500 gift certificate to a furniture or hardware store or a $1,000 vacation voucher to Las Vegas to a buyer who can close within 60 days. If you're making a $19,000 profit, you can afford to pay a rebate. Car companies and other marketers routinely offer rebates; why not you?
- Splitting the down payment. If it's legal and ethical, maybe you can pay the rebate up front to help the buyers with the down payment.

Wholesale buyers—that is, other investors—may find these alternatives appealing:

- Offering relatively low monthly payments with a short-term balloon (one to five years).
- Offering an easy monthly payment plan with lump-sum interval payments. Low monthly payments with larger amounts of cash due quarterly can help an investor pay the loan off in just one to three years. (Make sure the buyer can make the payments.)
- Offering a barter or exchange for other real estate.

CHAPTER 7

The Landlord Opportunity: Buying, Holding, and Renting Property

Bigness comes from doing many small things well.

—R. H. Macy

Flipping and rehabbing houses are great ways to make money, but there are not many millionaire flippers or rehabbers. Buying, holding, and renting, however, can be one of the best long-term wealth builders available. Many people have bought, held, and rented single-family houses, duplexes, and apartment buildings, paid off their debt with tenants' rent, and watched the value of their properties double and even triple over time.

You probably know someone who bought a house for $50,000 many years ago that is now worth $200,000. If you buy right and are willing to work with your properties and tenants over a long period of time, then you someday may have a similar story to tell your friends, children, or grandchildren.

If you find a great deal on a home, you may decide that holding it and renting it out is the best strategy. This provides good cash flow and allows your tenants to pay off your mortgage while building your wealth over the long term. In addition, because of all the deductions and depreciation you are allowed, the income that you earn will probably be nearly nontaxable. Be sure to consult your accountant.

Obviously, the downside of holding property is that you have to be a landlord. As a landlord, you really aren't in the business of renting property—you're in the business of solving problems for people. That may entail everything from finding the right people for your units to fixing leaky faucets in the middle of the night. If this doesn't sound like your kind of job, look for a professional property manager who can handle tenant concerns while you track down new deals. If you do decide to become a landlord, set up systems that will help solve problems for other people and yourself quickly, efficiently, and as with as little stress as possible. This chapter will help you start.

How to Be the Best Landlord

Every year businesses go belly up, leaving their owners wondering what went wrong. Meanwhile, a few small businesspeople keep thriving, many of them delivering profits beyond their owners' most optimistic dreams.

What makes the difference? Management, not luck. To succeed as a landlord, you need to be able to manage property and personalities. That means you need to be able to

- attract and keep responsible tenants who pay promptly;
- set up a good, tough, but fair, rent collection system;
- write formal policies and enforce them to the letter;
- inspect, maintain, and repair buildings;
- solve tenant problems and meet tenant needs; and
- evict tenants when necessary.

Treat landlording like a business: Be professional, not emotional. Establish clear policies and procedures, and stick to them. Set up a system for managing your properties. You must run the business—don't let the business run you!

Attract Responsible Tenants

The first three rules of renting are screen, screen, and screen your tenants! It's better to have an empty house for six months than to have one bad tenant. Responsible tenants will make your life easy; bad or irresponsible tenants can make it a nightmare. You want people who pay the rent on time, take care of your property, and stay a long time.

The search for good tenants begins with advertising. Large, easy-to-read yard signs that describe the property will draw attention. So will fliers and posters. When you advertise in the newspaper, use bold print, brackets, or a border of stars to set off your ad from the rest. Use phrases like "won't last" and "great landlord looking for great tenants." Include the location of the property and describe its amenities. If you have remodeled the property, say so.

Because good tenants and neighbors often know people just like themselves, I give them "wanted" posters that say "Wanted: Good tenants," and then describe the property. Promoting the unit to local employers and universities also will attract good people.

If you have several units for rent, use voice mail to describe the properties. You can order voice mail very inexpensively from your phone company. This will save you from repeating the same thing—description of the property, directions, amenities, when available—a hundred times. On the recording, you can give out your direct line.

Return all phone calls from potential tenants the same day. My places stay rented because I or my assistant return all calls. Many tenants tell me that they called dozens of places, but I was the first and only landlord to call back. I know the average person can make 30 to 40 calls an hour, so there's no reason not to get back to people right away. A simple return phone call will set you apart—and above—most other landlords.

When you call, get each person's name and phone number first. Then ask what the tenant is interested in. Describe all of the positive aspects of your unit. Details are important—mention carpet, miniblinds, washer-dryer hookups, ceiling fans, type of yard, location, and so forth. If you can't meet the person's needs—for example, your units are too small, too large, too expensive—ask him or her to pass the word around about what you have available, or to call back later when his or her needs change.

Never reveal ahead how much the rent is. Always ask, "How much are you looking to spend?" For example, you may want $575, but the tenant may want to spend $600. By letting the person go first, you either can agree to the higher price or raise their offer. Get at least what you want or more.

The million-dollar question to ask is: "Why are you moving?" Investigate the person's answer. Explain that you check references, and ask if their two previous landlords will give a good recommendation. If the person says no, ask why. There may be a legitimate reason.

Explain that you do a credit check on all applicants. Tell the person you have a little flexibility, so as not to scare him or her away, but ask: "What will I find?" This will prove useful later when you do a credit check to see if the person is truthful or not. Always check for truthfulness and stability. There are firms that will do this for you, or you can associate with your local credit bureau. You also can get very low-cost credit and background checks at my Web site, <www.shemin.com>.

If your conversation leaves you feeling good about the prospective tenants, arrange to show the apartment. First, ask the prospective tenants to drive by the property to see if they are interested and call you back if they want to see it. Then hold what I call a "renting party." If five people are interested in a property, I tell them all to meet me at the same time. Experience has taught me that if five people say they are coming, two or three will turn up. Scheduling them for the same time saves me the time and trouble of meeting people who never arrive—and it lets everyone know there is plenty of interest in the property. I also tell tenants that I only will wait five minutes for an appointment. And I make it a practice never to wait more than ten minutes for a latecomer.

Take a look at each tenant's car. I believe the way people maintain their cars predicts a lot about how they will maintain your property. I always bring candy for children. Some landlords bring along toys and watch how the children play and the families interact. This can be a good preview of how they will act in your place. I've actually had families start screaming and fighting with one another while they were looking at the apartment! Naturally, I didn't rent to them.

Whether you are talking by phone or meeting face to face, be cheerful, positive, and polite. Remember, you are selling your unit. Point out the benefits of the house and your ability to take care of tenants' needs. Show some interest in the prospective tenants and answer their questions. A friendly attitude automatically puts you in the top 2 percent of all landlords.

Never discuss the race of the neighborhoods. If someone asks, reply, "I don't know, I am color-blind." If a potential tenant asks about the crime rate in the neighborhood, respond with the truth and direct them to the local police department for more details. Try never to make any comments about safety or security, or they may come back to haunt you later in a lawsuit.

If the visit goes well and the prospect is interested, have him or her fill out an application. Before you decide to rent to the person, though, check their credit and all references very carefully.

ROBERT'S RULES

You run and control the business. Never let tenants run and control your time and business.

Retain Responsible Tenants

It can cost you five times more to get a new tenant than to keep the one you already have. When a tenant leaves, you may have to spend $500 to $1,500 repairing the unit, your property will be empty from 30 to 90 days, and you will need to spend time and money looking for a new tenant. I would rather spend $100 on a repair to keep a tenant than lose a tenant *and* three months of rent.

To keep my tenants happy, I have instituted a Recognition and Acknowledgment program (R&A). A human's longing for recognition and acknowledgment is powerful—often much greater than love and even stronger than hope. That's why it's important to constantly pursue ways to make your tenants and prospective tenants feel extra special.

Let them feel that you're interested in them not just because they're tenants, but because they're human beings in whom you have a deep and abiding interest. If you're sincere and persistent in your efforts, you'll have an effective advantage over others in real estate.

In fact, your basic employee and tenant policies must foster living and breathing tender loving care (TLC) techniques. TLC can do wonders to persuade an irresponsible tenant to your side and help ensure that your tenants pay their rent on time and take good care of your property.

Providing TLC is not just a one-shot, one-tenant event. It's a process that has to be sustained day in and day out. To make it work means you have to be fanatical about every transaction, every hour of every day. It means responding to a tenant's complaint in a timely manner. It means treating every tenant with courtesy. It means not feeling that you're above eating lunch with a low-cost housing tenant. It means treating everyone you're involved with fairly, yet firmly.

You want to tell your responsible tenants that they are valued and that you are sympathetic to their needs. You want them to know that you'll be there when they need you, and that your commitment is ongoing. When this is your attitude, many of your responsible tenants will bring even more responsible referrals.

One way to convey recognition and acknowledgment is to give responsible tenants more than they expect. I try to provide rewards that residents appreciate, such as fresh paint, borders to rooms, ceiling fans, and brass plates (interestingly enough, most tenants are willing to pay for new wallpaper and curtains to match). Set up a schedule of rewards. For example, offer free carpet cleaning or a ceiling fan to tenants who pay on time after they've stayed for a year. Tenants who have completed two years may receive brass kickplates or another ceiling fan. After three years, you could offer a $200 credit toward the home improvement of their choice. Figure the profit over the tenants' lifetime to get an idea of what you can afford to spend to keep them. Gifts like these stay with the property and add real value. (Make certain your tenants understand that the gift is for their living enjoyment as long as they stay with you; if they leave, the gift stays with the property.)

You don't need to spend a lot of money to make a tenant feel good. Sometimes, a simple, sincere gesture in the form of a thank-you note is sufficient to warm the cockles of even the most irresponsible tenant. Acknowledging birthdays and anniversaries is another way to get personal. All you need to do is get this information from your tenants and keep a revolving file that automatically triggers a specific letter. Sure, this takes time, but remember, tenants are your bread and butter—or did you forget who makes it possible for you to eat well on a regular basis?

One of the best times to start telling people that you appreciate them is during a holiday season. I like to do so at Thanksgiving, when a "thank you" is quite appropriate. You don't have to be a brilliant poet to recognize and acknowledge your responsible tenants.

Here's an example of a simple thank-you note:

Dear _____ ,

My wife, _____ , our daughter (see enclosed photos), and I were out shopping the other evening, and we decided to look for an appropriate Seasons Greetings card for you. However, because this is such a personal time of the year, instead of sending you a customary holiday card, I thought it may be more meaningful if I expressed how I feel about having you as a tenant.

First, I want you to know that I have a high regard for you as a special human being. I feel very fortunate to have you as a tenant. To have the opportunity to know and care for you is a trust I take very seriously. I hope you know that, in the event of any emergency, you can count on me to be there for you at an instant's notice.

You know, it seems that life's richest prizes (and I'm not talking about money) go to the man or woman who values good relationships. I think we all strive to nurture relationships that we can count on to be there when we are in need. As surely as a magnetized piece of steel draws to itself every bit of iron within reach, so does this same force in people draw them closer together when one needs support in emergency situations.

I want to thank you for being a truly responsible tenant, and express my sincere thanks for allowing me to be part of your extended family.

As my holiday gift to you, I've enclosed a gift certificate to _____ .

Have a blessed holiday season and a healthy and good new year.

Sincerely,

Your Name

Observe how intimate this letter is. Would the tenant know that I would be there in the event of an emergency situation (not just a minor problem)? Wouldn't it prevent the tenant from ever thinking of damaging his or her unit? Wouldn't it prevent the responsible tenant from dropping me as a landlord (what other landlord in the world sends out a letter like this)?

In today's tumultuous, highly competitive business environment, you have to be different and innovative in order to succeed. You have to develop yourself into a TLC personality so that people can identify with you. Often, that requires a top-to-bottom attitude adjustment from the landlord down to the garbage hauler.

You must think of each and every tenant as a long-term investment. It's the profit to you over the tenant's lifetime that's important. A regular R&A program can mean that a tenant will stay with you for a long, long time.

For those whose greed glands don't buy this "pampering-the-tenant-within-reason" concept, I ask you again to think in terms of the hard dollars you'll lose in rent if you treat your tenants shabbily. Moreover, it's a fact of life that if you don't treat your tenants well, you'll get exactly what you deserve: irresponsible tenants (and their irresponsible friends, significant others, and the like) who could damage your property. You should follow the R&A program. It's good business, and more importantly, it's the right thing to do.

If you do what's right for your tenants, you'll begin to receive letters (some will make great testimonials) that you can use when you're interviewing prospective tenants, or when you're applying for a loan, or when you approach a nonprofit group with a joint venture proposal. Those testimonials can go a long way to keep your units occupied so you'll have more demand for your property than you can ever hope to handle. And that translates into a perpetual source of revenue.

 R O B E R T ' S   R U L E S

Three-Day Rent Repair Policy

The leading tenant complaint is that landlords don't do repairs as promised. To prevent those complaints and set yourself apart from other landlords, try a "three-day rent repair" policy. If a tenant calls or writes to request a repair, I take care of it within three business days or else I pay the tenant a day's rent in cash for each day until the repair is complete.

This policy tells tenants that I am serious about repairs and helps keep my properties in good repair and rented! I tell prospective tenants about this policy when they inspect an apartment, although most of them forget about my promise because they know they can count on me. But once or twice I've failed to meet my deadline and had to pay up. You can believe they were very impressed!

Collect Delinquent Rent and Evict Tenants for Nonpayment

As a landlord, unless you follow some pretty hard and fast rules, the toughest variable to control is your emotions. And the hardest job is this: Don't fall for the hard luck stories of those who miss a rent payment.

A missed rent payment is not an occasion to become lax. It's a time to stick to your guns. Once tenants get behind, they rarely ever catch up! I don't have to tell you that once tenants find you to be a pushover on delinquent rent, it doesn't take too long for the word to get around. And what that attracts are irresponsible tenants—who can crowd out the responsible people in no time flat.

My policy is that all rent is due on the first of every month, and is delinquent (with fees due) on the 5th. More fees accrue on the 10th of the month, and eviction proceedings begin on the 16th. Every city and state is different, so check with a local real estate attorney or real estate association before you set your own policy and procedure. Establish a written policy, and make sure tenants read and sign it before they move in. Be very businesslike and polite to all tenants who are late on their rent. Listen to their excuses, but don't acknowledge them. Tell them that your collection processes are business policy, set forth by the owner of the property, and that there are no exceptions. Explain that if they don't pay the rent in a timely fashion, their credit will be marked and they will be turned over to a collection attorney. Use neutral language, but be firm. You could say something like the following:

> The computer shows that your rent payment is now delinquent. And when that happens we never, and I mean never, waver from the rental agreement that you signed. I'm sorry you're having difficulties paying the rent. But as the rental agreement says, you must keep up with the rent no matter what. By signing this agreement you made that pledge. It is one rule that we must enforce or we'd be out of business.

Occasionally I have to evict someone for not paying rent. Even though I am an attorney, I hire an attorney to do my evictions and collections. It is very unpleasant to have to evict someone, and the laws can be very complicated, so let a professional handle it for you. These professionals have a better chance of actually collecting the money owed you, and you will know the procedure was handled correctly.

Once you turn over a tenant to an attorney for eviction, you no longer can communicate with him or her. The tenant also cannot bother you. Start the procedure by notifying the tenant in writing that you will turn the matter over, on such and such a date, to your eviction attorney. Let the person know you do not want to do this, but it is your policy and procedure.

To find a good eviction attorney who is knowledgeable about the process in your area, call your local real estate association or apartment association, or ask local property managers. You can also visit my Web site, <www.shemin.com>, to find out how you can get a top attorney in your area—at a substantial discount—to answer your questions, review your paperwork, and do your evictions.

Use Lease-Optioning to Benefit You and Your Tenants

Lease-optioning (see Chapter 1) is an excellent tool for landlords. In a lease-purchase, you negotiate a long-term lease with a tenant, and give him or her an option to purchase the property. If a house is valued at $65,000 (and presuming you purchased it for much less), you might lease-option the property to Wanda Tenant for $1,000 option money, $750 per month rent, and an option to buy the property for $65,000, all good for two years. A portion of her monthly rent, perhaps $100, goes toward her down payment.

I believe you are always better off lease-optioning a property than renting it. Let's compare the two arrangements side by side:

Renting	*Lease-Optioning*
Security deposit is refundable; you are holding tenants' money.	Option money is not refundable, even if optioners choose not to buy; not taxable until option is exercised or expires.
There is no pride of ownership.	There is pride of ownership— tenants may own it someday.
Little incentive to pay rent on time.	Great incentive to pay on time if contract states that option money and payments will be forfeited if rent is paid late.

Renters move often.	People contemplating buying the house will stay.
Rent is at the market rate.	Rent can be slightly higher than market rate because the lease purchasers have the right to purchase the house and you are offering them a much-needed service.
You are responsible for repairs.	You can make the lease purchasers responsible for repairs (if legal in your state—check with your attorney).

I ask all my new tenants if they want to lease-option, because I know my property will be better cared for and I won't have to bother with the kind of piddly but expensive repairs that drive a landlord crazy. I'll cut down on property management headaches, increase my cash flow, and decrease my repair expenses. I'll also get more money up front, and I will get to keep it! I do this with single-family houses and with duplexes when I have an investor who would like to buy the whole building.

In fact, you can start right now with the tenants you currently rent to. Explain to them that you're going to help them buy their home. Get as large a deposit from the lease purchaser as possible. You can use part of the rent they pay as an incentive toward a down payment, but only if it's on time. This probably will cause them to pay their rent on time more consistently—especially if your agreement states that if they don't pay on time, they'll lose their deposit and their down payment savings.

Lease-purchasing is becoming easier to understand as the "rent to own" concept takes on. People rent to own cars and furniture, so why not housing? It's a win-win situation. If you bought the property at a 25 to 30 percent discount, you will profit greatly if you sell it to a tenant at full retail value. Tenants also benefit—especially those with minor credit problems or some debts who might not otherwise be able to become homeowners. The option arrangement gives them time to clean up their problems, and helps them set aside money every month toward the down payment.

Always use separate lease and option agreements. If you have to evict the tenant, you can go to court with the lease. If the option is attached to a part of the lease, a judge may deem the agreement to be a purchase and not rule in your favor for a timely eviction.

Lease-Optioning and the Landlord Challenge

Because I believe that businesspeople should use part of their business or time to help others, I use lease-optioning at least once each year to help a homeless family acquire one of my rental properties. They must have a job and a desire to better themselves. During the year, I help the family to budget, improve their credit, and encourage them to take a home ownership class at a local bank or nonprofit community organization.

At the end of the year, I help them to get a new loan or mortgage so that they can buy the home from me. Because most people have trouble coming up with a down payment on a house, I help them save for the down payment by escrowing their rent for a year. I also let them buy the house at a substantial discount so that they, not I, benefit from "the good deal." To find out more about helping others in real estate, visit my Web site <www.shemin.com>.

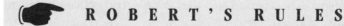

ROBERT'S RULES

Whatever you do or whatever business you are in, take some of your time or money and help others. Not only will you be helping someone less fortunate, but you will be helping yourself and your business.

Set Policies and Procedures

You must have a written set of policies and procedures if you are to run any business successfully. Landlording is no different. Even the term "landlord" may not be professional, because many tenants have a negative image of it. Very few people say they want to grow up to be a landlord. Your first policy should be to distinguish yourself and perhaps use a term coined by the Real Estate Investors of Cincinnati and the Ohio Real Estate Investors Association—"Professional Housing Provider."

You should never landlord unless all your policies and procedures are in writing. The benefit of having written policies and procedures is that you will never or rarely have any stress or decision making associated with your properties, because everything has already been decided in your policies. Take some time now to write your policy manual and keep your finished policies and procedures in an easily accessible notebook. Feel free to use, change, or adapt some of mine.

The basic property management duties and responsibilities that your policies and procedures should cover include the following:

- Collecting rent
- Issuing late notices by the 10th of each month
- Depositing all rental income
- Rent rolls
- Calling tenants on the 10th to remind them about the rent
- Bookkeeping
  - Generating reports on all properties by the 15th of the month
  - Completing payroll
  - Paying all mortgages, bills, etc., in a timely fashion
  - Filing and general office management
- Prospecting for tenants
- Answering all rental calls promptly (same day) and following up to make sure tenant is satisfied
  - Treating rental calls as sales calls
  - Maintaining a list of potential tenants
- Coordinating Section 8 initial and annual inspections, leases, etc. (Section 8 is discussed in detail in Chapter 8.)
- Resolving tenant complaints
- Drawing up new leases and lease renewals
- Establishing new rental rates
- Terminating tenants when necessary

Here are some other policies I would recommend you practice as a landlord:

- Keep all information on each of your tenants on one sheet of paper in a notebook. Include their name, address, phone number, rent amount, deposit amount, and move-in date.

- Inspect all of your properties every 30 days. You should do this so you can spot problems early on and deal with them. It also shows tenants that you are serious about your property. Let tenants know in writing and have them sign a permission slip that you can and will inspect filters and heating and cooling units, and spray for bugs, for example, on the second Tuesday of every month between 8 AM and 5 PM.
- Never give a key to anyone to move into or repair any of your units without first doing a credit and criminal background check. However, you must get written permission to do a credit or background check on anyone. Use their application fee or, if they are going to be a contractor, deduct the fee from the cost of the job. If they will not let you, do not let them move into or repair any of the units. These procedures are very reasonable, and they are a must. Visit my Web site <www.shemin.com> for some referrals.
- Charge for any and all tenant damage. Tenant damage becomes part of the rent due. If it is not paid, then the rent is not paid, and the tenant can be evicted.

Policies and Procedures for Contractors

I would recommend the following policies and procedures for contractors who work on your properties—with no exceptions:

- All contracts must be in writing and as detailed as possible.
- No checks will be issued without written contracts and invoices.
- Regarding draws, a maximum of ⅓ (one-third) of the total bid will be given up front to cover materials. The balance will not be paid until all work is absolutely complete. If one doorknob is loose or one sink has a small leak, the balance will not be paid.
- The balance will not be paid until all of the contractor's trash is removed.
- Service calls will not be paid until they are completed and verified by the tenant that they are complete.

- Contractor will give a date for the completion of a job. If the job is not complete by said date, and the landlord loses money by not being able to rent out the property, then a $50 per day penalty will be deducted from the contractor's final draw for each day, including weekends, that the job is not done.
- On houses for Section 8, 20 percent of the total will be held back until the unit passes the Section 8 inspection.
- A $25 bonus will be paid for units that pass the Section 8 inspection the first time.
- Contractor will guarantee work for six months. (Just like everything, get it in writing.)
- Contractor must show proof of workers' compensation insurance. If not, the premiums will be deducted from the cost of the job and paid by the owner or property manager.

I have all contractors sign and agree to these policies and procedures, as well as one regarding liability that clarifies the contractor's status as a contractor and not an employee.

CHAPTER 8

Section 8 Housing:
A Profitable Strategy

You can come to expect that which you inspect regularly.

–Heisenberg's Principle

As a landlord concentrating in lower- and moderate-income neighborhoods, I have many tenants who participate in the federal Section 8 housing program.

The Section 8 Program assists eligible people by paying a portion of their rent to a private owner. The program is funded by the Department of Housing and Urban Development (HUD) and applied by your state housing development agency (human resource agency or city housing agency).

Eligible applicants must be a member of a family (two or more persons related by blood, marriage, or with evidence of a stable family relationship); or age 62 or older; or disabled if under age 62; or a single, eligible person; and cannot have an outstanding debt to a public housing agency. The applicant's gross annual income must fall below the income limits set by HUD. Most Section 8 certificate and voucher holders are single mothers, elderly, and/or disabled people.

The Section 8 housing program is so popular that in most towns and cities there is a long waiting list of persons applying for assistance.

A steady stream of tenants plus government-guaranteed rent makes the Section 8 program very attractive to landlords. Not having to collect rent is certainly appealing to me! Like any government program, the Section 8 housing program is complex. I encountered plenty of paperwork when I first entered the program, but now it runs like clockwork.

This chapter offers a primer on the Section 8 housing program. Use it to decide whether participating as a landlord will benefit you, too. The Section 8 program does change from time to time; check with your local housing authority for the most recent rules and regulations.

 R O B E R T ' S   R U L E S

Here are nine powerful wealth-building reasons to concentrate your landlording efforts in the low-cost, subsidized housing area:

1. Government will pay all or most of your rent.

2. Rent is guaranteed for 12 months with Section 8. No bounced checks!

3. Tax consequences are excellent.

4. Cash flow can be controlled if you buy right.

5. Capital appreciation is excellent.

6. Diversification reduces risk.

7. Depreciation is a powerful factor.

8. Tax credits may be available and can be held or sold for almost instant income.

9. You can get some of the best deals in real estate in low- to moderate-income housing.

Section 8 Housing Questions and Answers

Q. What types of properties qualify for Section 8 certification?

A. A family may choose an apartment, a duplex, a single-family house, or a mobile home. To be the correct size for the family, a unit must have one bedroom for every two occupants. It may not be owner occupied. The unit must be in good condition and pass an inspection. The inspection determines compliance with HUD's housing quality standards, summarized on pages 154–56.

Q. How does an owner determine that a family is eligible for Section 8?

A. Before it can begin to look for a unit of housing, a family must be issued a certificate or voucher stating that it is eligible and shows the period of time it has to search for a housing unit, usually 60 days. If an acceptable unit cannot be found before the certificate or voucher expires, it is given to the next person on the waiting list.

Note: An owner always should contact the local HUD office before making any commitment to a family. The unit must pass inspection, and a lease and contract must be signed before the family moves into the unit and before subsidy payments may begin.

Q. Is there much paperwork for an owner?

A. The owner must sign one lease with the tenant. The owner may use the state's HUD model lease or his or her own lease with a HUD addendum. (The owner may not have a tenant sign more than one lease.) The owner must also sign a contract with the local HUD office that authorizes the payments to the owner. The local staff prepares the lease and contract.

Q. How much rent may an owner charge?

A. The amount of rent that may be charged is limited by the fair market rent for the particular county and bedroom size. Fair market rents are set by HUD. The amount paid for rent to the owner, plus utilities, may not exceed the fair market rent.

Note: The family is not allowed to make up any difference between what an owner is asking and the amount allowed by the fair market rent. In addition, the rent the owner charges also must be comparable to similar unassisted units in the same neighborhood. And the owner may not charge more to rent a Section 8 unit than he or she would to rent the unit to a private, unassisted tenant.

Q. Does the tenant pay any of the rent?

A. Under the program, tenants pay according to their income. Families generally pay no more than 30 percent of their monthly adjusted income.

Q. Who pays the utilities?

A. This arrangement is negotiated between the landlord and tenant and specified in the lease. Regardless of who pays, every unit must have electricity; an adequate, acceptable, permanent heat source; running water; hot water; a stove; and a refrigerator.

I recommend that the tenants pay their own utilities when possible. It is difficult to control utility usage. Of course, if the landlord pays, they are allowed to charge higher rent.

Q. Who chooses the tenants?

A. Section 8 staff are responsible for determining if an applicant is eligible for the subsidy, but they don't screen applicants as potential tenants. Screening for desirable tenants is the responsibility of the owner. An owner doesn't have to accept tenants simply because they hold a certificate or voucher. You as a landlord should and must screen all tenants.

Q. How often are inspections done?

A. The unit must pass an inspection before the tenant moves in. If the tenant currently occupies the unit, it must pass the inspection before the tenant is admitted to the program. After the initial inspection, subsequent inspections are done every 12 months for as long as the unit remains on the program. Special inspections may be done if the owner or tenant requests it, or as part of an audit.

It is the owner's responsibility to make all repairs and to maintain the unit so it always passes housing quality standards. Rental payments may be abated for any period in which a unit does not pass housing quality standards.

If a tenant damages a unit or takes action that causes the unit not to pass housing quality standards, it is the owner's responsibility to make any needed repairs or corrections. The owner may bill and/or evict the tenant for tenant damages.

Q. How long is a family eligible for assistance?

A. A family is certified as eligible for a 12-month period, and must be recertified every 12 months, also called the anniversary date. If a family's eligibility has not been recertified before the anniversary date, the payments automatically stop at the end of the twelfth month. Payments are resumed as soon as eligibility is recertified.

A family may continue receiving assistance as long as it continues to be eligible, and the unit continues to pass housing quality standards. If a family vacates a unit, the payment of that unit stops. The owner should always notify the agent if the family vacates.

If a family's assistance is terminated because of fraud, its failure to cooperate, or excessive income, the landlord is notified that assistance will stop. If the landlord agrees, the family may remain in the unit and pay all of the rent itself.

Q. May an owner evict a Section 8 tenant?

A. An owner may evict a tenant under the terms of the lease. The owner must follow state and local laws of eviction.

Q. Are rental increases allowed?

A. An owner may request a rental increase every 12 months at the time of the contract anniversary date. The amount of the increase is controlled by adjustment factors published by HUD. In addition, the rental increase may be given only if the new rent will be comparable to that of other nonassisted units in the same neighborhood.

An owner who desires a rental increase must make the request in writing to the agent at least 60 days prior to the contract anniversary date. The owner's request should include how much of an increase is desired and the reason(s) the increase is requested. Acceptable reasons include increased taxes, increased utility bills, or property improvements. Verification should be provided on all three reasons. The agent will notify the owner of the amount of the increase.

The agent may refuse an increase if an owner has failed to maintain the property, if there appears to be no justification for an increase, or if comparable nonassisted units rent for less.

Q. Does the tenant's portion of the rent ever change?

A. The amount the tenant pays may change during the year if the family's income or composition changes. The owner is notified in writing of any such changes and it is then the owner's responsibility to collect the tenant's portion of the rent. An owner may evict a tenant who does not pay his or her portion of the rent. Many tenants on Section 8 have all of their rent paid for by the government directly to you. Unpaid tenant rent may be collectible as damages.

Q. Is an owner eligible to collect the rental subsidy payment once a tenant moves?

A. No. When a tenant vacates a unit or dies, the contract and lease become void. Any checks received after the tenant vacates should be returned.

Q. What about unpaid tenant rent and tenant damages?

A. If tenants do not pay their portion of the rent, an owner should begin eviction proceedings. If a tenant damages a unit, the owner must make the repairs. The agent should be contacted prior to making the repairs. The owner should then bill the tenants for the repairs. If there are unpaid tenant damages and/or rent after tenants vacate a unit, the owner may apply for reimbursement for these items. How much is paid depends on whether the tenant held a voucher or a certificate. For specific details, see the section entitled "Procedures for Filing Claims" later in this chapter.

Q. When and how does an owner get the rental money each month?

A. The owner is responsible for collecting the tenant's portion of the rent. This should be collected on the first of every month. An owner may designate late charges; however, these late charges must be stated as an addendum to the lease.

The agency's portion of the rent is mailed on the first working day of each month for the following month. Any adjustment monies or amounts owed for prior months are sent on special checks. The check automatically will be stopped at the end of the contract anniversary day if the renewal process has not been completed. Once the renewal is received and processed by the agency, the payments resume. The first check for a new tenant may take six to eight weeks because a file must be established in the state's computer system before it can be issued.

Q. How does an owner become a Section 8 landlord?

A. Contact the local Section 8 staff in your area for information. The program is most likely administered by your state or city housing agency.

Q. Can an owner sell property occupied by a Section 8 tenant?

A. An owner must coordinate the sale of the property with the local staff. The seller should advise the buyer of the Section 8 obligation and turn over any security deposits held for the tenant. The buyer also must be willing to honor the Section 8 lease and contract.

Q. What are the advantages of being a Section 8 landlord?

A. Advantages include the following:

- A portion of the rent is guaranteed and comes in like clockwork every month. There are no bounced checks, which could be a real problem with some low-cost housing tenants.
- There is some reimbursement for unpaid tenant rent.
- There is some reimbursement for damages.
- It's an area of housing that many real estate people avoid or ignore—which means less competition for you.
- There is potential for excellent cash flow, capital appreciation, and depreciation.
- Distressed housing that can be rehabbed can dramatically increase your bottom line.

Q. What are the responsibilities and obligations as a Section 8 landlord?

A. Responsibilities include the following:

- To manage routine functions such as screening and selecting tenants, maintaining the property, collecting rent, and handling tenant problems. Participation in the program does not relieve a landlord of any normal duties. The program simply pays all or a portion of the tenant's rent.
- To comply with all the requirements contained in the lease and agency contract.

- To maintain the unit at all times so it always passes HUD's housing quality standards. (See summary of Housing Quality Standards on pages 154–56.) Owners are responsible for repairs even if damages are caused by the tenant, though the tenant may be charged for any damages they caused. Eviction also may be considered for tenant damage.
- To collect only the amount of rent from the tenant that is specified in the lease or agency contract or any interim adjustment notices. Any charges in addition to the monthly rent must be stated in the lease or lease addendum.
- To notify the local staff if a tenant is being evicted, and follow state and local laws governing eviction.
- To notify the local representative immediately if the tenant vacates the unit. Landlords are not eligible to receive rental payments if the tenant is not living in the unit and the agency contract automatically terminates if the tenant leaves the unit. Any rental payments received following the month the tenant vacates the unit is to be returned to the agency.
- To notify the local staff and tenant at least 60 days prior to the lease anniversary date if a rental increase is requested for the next year.
- To comply with all HUD/agency requirements in order to be eligible to file claims for tenant damages, unpaid rent, or vacancy loss. (See "Procedures for Filing Claims" on page 157.)
- To immediately report to the local staff if any utilities are disconnected, whether paid for by the tenant or landlord. If a tenant or landlord fails to fulfill the obligation to connect/pay utilities as outlined in the lease, rental subsidy will be abated and/or terminated.
- To provide proof of ownership of a unit.
- To provide a W-9 for purposes of filing a correct 1099 with the IRS.

Failure to fulfill these obligations and requirements may result in the withholding, abatement, or termination of housing assistance payments. Future participation in the programs may be prohibited.

Minimum Housing Quality Standards

The following checklist summarizes the housing quality standards that a rental unit must meet. While standards vary from area to area, they generally require that a unit be safe, clean, and up to codes/standards. For a more detailed explanation of housing quality standards, request a copy of the HUD Handbook for Administering the Section 8 Program.

No lease or contract should ever be signed until a unit meets housing quality standards. It is the landlord's responsibility to maintain the unit so it always meets these standards. If a tenant causes a unit to become substandard, the landlord must make the necessary repairs. The landlord may bill the tenant for the repairs or initiate eviction proceedings if appropriate.

When a landlord endorses the housing assistance payment each month, he or she is certifying that the unit meets housing quality standards. If HUD or its representatives determine that a unit is substandard and the landlord refuses to make the necessary repairs within a designated period of time, the housing assistance payment may be abated or canceled.

Housing Quality Standards Checklist

Interior

❏ All units must have private access without going through any other unit's living area. All units must have sufficient access and egress to provide an alternative means of escape in case of fire.

❏ The unit must have a separate living area, kitchen, bathroom, and one bedroom for each two persons.

❏ The living room must have two electrical outlets in working condition. An overhead light may be considered as one outlet. The living room must have a window. If the window was designed to be opened, it must be operable.

❏ The kitchen must have one electrical outlet and an overhead light in working condition. It must have a stove and refrigerator in good, workable condition. These two items may be furnished by the tenant or landlord. There must be adequate space for storage and a sink with hot and cold running water. The sink cannot have leaks and must have a proper drain trap.

❑ The bathroom must have a toilet, tub or shower, and a sink. All fixtures must be workable, without leaks, and with proper drain traps. The bathroom must have an exterior, operable window or a vent. There must be one permanently installed light fixture.

❑ All bedrooms must have two workable electric outlets. An overhead light may be considered as one outlet. The bedrooms must each have an exterior window.

❑ The unit must be free of bugs, mice, rats, and other vermin.

❑ All units must have a fire alarm or smoke detector in working condition on each level.

Plumbing, Heating, and Electricity

❑ All electrical wiring must be safe. Cover plates must be on all outlets, and there must not be any frayed or exposed wiring.

❑ All utilities must be connected by the landlord or the tenant. A unit without utilities is considered substandard.

❑ There must be a permanent heat source in safe, operating condition. Unvented space heaters, kerosene heaters, and portable electric heaters should not be considered as the permanent heat source. The heat system must be capable of providing heat directly or indirectly to all rooms used for living.

❑ Each unit must have a properly installed and operating hot water heater with a temperature and pressure sensitive relief valve. There must be a discharge line pointing toward the floor or drained to the exterior of the unit. Gas water heaters must be properly vented.

❑ The water and sewer system must be served by an approved public or private system.

❑ All plumbing must be free of leaks or corrosion and be properly vented.

Windows and Doors

❑ All operable windows must have locks. Windows must be unbroken, secure, and weather-tight.

❑ All exterior doors must be secure, weather-tight, and lockable.

❑ All glass in windows and doors must be unbroken and free of cracks.

❑ Each room used for sleeping or living that has one or more windows made to be opened must have a screen on at least one window, unless the unit has central air-conditioning.

Interior and Exterior Surfaces and Steps

❑ All interior and exterior surfaces of the unit must be free of cracked, peeling paint.

❑ All steps (interior and exterior) of four or more must have handrails, possibly on both sides.

❑ All interior and exterior surfaces, including the walls, floors, ceilings, roofs, and foundations must be free of holes, cracks, leaks, and other deterioration that would pose a hazard or allow wind or rain into the unit.

Exterior

❑ The roof and gutters must be free of defects that allow air or water infiltration.

❑ All entrances to crawl spaces should be covered, and exterior vents should be covered with screens.

❑ All porches and balconies higher than 30 inches off the ground must have rails designed so a child may not crawl through them, and sturdy enough to support a person who might be falling.

❑ All mobile homes must have tie downs.

❑ The yard must be free of debris, garbage, trash, etc.

Procedures for Filing Claims

Claims for damages. HUD and many local and state agencies have changed the procedures for collecting damages against Section 8 tenants. Of course, you can try to collect and sue a Section 8 tenant for damage just as you would any other tenant. Remember, you only can charge for damage they or their guests did. You cannot charge them for "normal" wear and tear, such as wear on the carpet, after they have been there seven years. Please check with your local city and/or state housing authority to find out all the details of your Section 8 program.

Claims for unpaid rent. Collecting rent is the landlord's responsibility, not the responsibility of the agency or its staff. A landlord should not allow a tenant to accumulate a large unpaid rent debt, because although you may file a claim with the Section 8 program, there is a limit on the amount that may be reimbursed. It is the landlord's responsibility to evict a tenant for nonpayment of rent.

If a tenant vacates a unit owing unpaid rent, a landlord first must attempt to collect the rent from the tenant. Proof of this attempt must accompany the claim, which also must include an itemized statement showing the months and amounts of unpaid rent. If only a partial claim is paid, the landlord may continue efforts to collect from the tenant.

Claims for vacancy loss. The landlord must immediately notify the Section 8 staff of a vacancy loss if a tenant with a certificate moved in violation of the lease. The landlord must sign and submit the HUD claim form furnished by the Section 8 staff within 60 days of the vacancy. If a damage claim is filed, the unit also must be inspected.

The landlord must make every effort to rent the unit. Proof of this effort, such as copies of newspaper ads, must accompany a claim. Attempts to rent the unit may include making it available to other certificate or voucher holders who are looking. The landlord must notify the Section 8 staff of the date the unit is rented.

A landlord who evicts a tenant may apply for vacancy loss only if he or she complied with the terms of the agency contract and lease and all applicable laws.

Payment for vacancy will be made as follows:

- For the month the tenant vacated the unit, the owner will receive the housing assistance payment due under the contract for as much of the month as the unit remains vacant.
- If the unit remains vacant after the month the vacancy occurred, the landlord may claim a housing assistance payment in the amount of 80 percent of the contract rent for a vacancy period not to exceed one additional month, or the expiration of the lease, whichever comes first. Any amounts paid by the tenant, including any remaining security deposit, will be deducted from the payment to the landlord. If the unit is rented the month following the vacancy, the vacancy loss payment will be paid only for the vacant days.

Preventing claims is much easier than pursuing claims. Screen carefully and only select solid, responsible tenants. Make regular inspections of each unit. (This is not the Section 8 staff's job!) Deal with tenant problems immediately. If a tenant is damaging a unit or not paying the required portion of the rent, take action quickly.

Working with Contractors on Section 8 Housing

When I use contractors to repair or improve Section 8 housing, I hold back 20 percent of the job total until the unit passes the Section 8 inspection. I also pay a $25 bonus for units that pass the Section 8 inspection the first time. I recommend the following when working with contractors:

- The contractor's work must be guaranteed for six months.
- Always retain first right of refusal, that is, a bidder who agrees to perform work will not be permitted to subcontract to another party without written permission first.
- The bidder must be on the job site either working on the project or overseeing his or her employees.
- The bidder is an independent agent and alone has the responsibility and liability for his or her workers.
- Never write or mail a check without having a proper invoice.

CHAPTER 9

Succeeding in Real Estate

Luck is where preparation meets opportunity.

—Anonymous

While it is possible to get rich quick, it's highly unlikely. I had many successes in the first six months I got into real estate, but it took about two years to really hit my stride. I got where I am today by taking a long-term approach to my business.

To succeed, commit to your business for the long term. Set and strive to meet long-term goals. Initiate systems that help you manage your business. Pursuing multiple real estate deals is complex, and it takes a well thought out system to manage them.

This chapter will reveal how to get started in the business, and how to manage your real estate investment business for long-term success.

Four-Week Action Plan for Launching a Real Estate Business

Most people who want to get into real estate investing stumble over one of two obstacles:

1. Some people get so much information about investing that they are overwhelmed and never get around to actually doing anything because it seems too complicated.

2. Others find the same information exciting, but they simply don't act. Their excuse is that they don't know how to start!

Obstacle number one tripped me up when I began. I spent six months stuck in the grip of "paralysis of analysis." I just looked, looked, looked; thought, thought, thought; and worried, worried, worried!

Finally, I realized something important: In most businesses, success stems from activity. To make money, you have to *do* something. The most successful real estate investors generally do more than those who are less successful. There are no big secrets or mysteries here. To succeed in real estate, you need to get busy.

The following action plan gives you simple things you can do each week for the next month. Do them consistently and persistently, and you'll learn a lot. In just a matter of weeks, you'll be ready to try your first couple of real estate deals. But don't rush. Take your time. Get good information. Seek the advice of investors and mentors who can show you the ropes. And then act!

Week One

❑ Call your Department of Housing and Urban Development (HUD) and Department of Veterans Affairs (VA) office to get lists of all properties for sale, if any, and look at four HUD or VA properties over the next four weeks.

❑ Begin to collect and update all of your financial data: savings, income, assets, and expenses. Request a copy of your credit report and find your tax returns.

❑ Look in the Sunday paper each and every Sunday. Circle all FSBO properties and all investment properties. Call on owners, talk to sellers, and look and learn.

Week Two

❑ Take two hours on Saturday to find an area of town that is "in transition" (not a great neighborhood, not a horrible neighborhood, but one that is being fixed up) and drive around it. Copy all FSBO signs, take down names and numbers from at least five real estate agent For Sale signs, and call those people. Look at at least five houses in the neighborhood. See what the houses look like; estimate their value, and start attempting to determine which ones are undervalued. Repeat this every Saturday for four weeks.

❏ Contact three real estate agents from three large companies. Tell them you are looking for undervalued properties that can either be fixed up and sold or fixed up and rented out. Also ask them for nonqualifying loans on houses. Have each of them show you at least five properties in the next five weeks.

❏ Call the local tax assessor's office. Find out when the next tax sale will be. Learn all you can about the tax sale and attend one tax sale auction in the next year.

❏ Call an attorney and find out in what publications foreclosures are publicized in in your area. Obtain and study at least one of these publications to help you understand and analyze the fore-closure notices.

❏ Call one major bank, one major mortgage company, and one second mortgage company and find the right person in the real estate owned (REO) department or special asset department to ask about real estate for sale. Contact the appropriate lending institutions in the next three weeks and get their lists of properties.

❏ Join your local real estate investment club.

❏ Attend two auctions this month. They are advertised in the real estate section of your paper, or call local auction companies and get on their mailing lists.

❏ At the auctions, meet at least two other real estate investors. Get their phone numbers, fax numbers, and addresses, and make note of the types of properties they buy. Take them out to lunch and ask them about their businesses and whether they'll show you some of their properties. You'll be amazed at what they'll reveal to you.

❏ Find two good and reputable contractors in your local area. Get to know them. Find out about all of their skills. Try to enlist them as bird dogs, offering them rewards when you close on a deal they found.

❏ Enlist at least three bird dogs in the next six weeks.

Week Three

❏ Put together a nice-looking financial package that includes your financial statement, résumé, etc. Make it look, feel, and be impressive.

Week Four

❏ Have a bank review your financial package. Ask for feedback.

❏ Review and fill out a sample land trust.

❏ Review and fill out two sample real estate contracts. You can get copies from your local Board of Agents, a real estate agent, and/or a real estate attorney. Compare them to the contracts in this book.

❏ Get a free initial consultation with an attorney to discuss how you should title your property. If you are going to be a landlord, also find out whether you need a property management company.

❏ Meet with your accountant within three weeks to discuss the tax implications of using a land trust, limited partnership, or corporation.

❏ Make ·five extremely low offers, presented in contract form, with your weasel clause and 90 days to close in the next 10 days. Make sure they are *low* offers, and review Chapters 3, 4, and 5 on analyzing, controlling, and financing properties.

❏ If you and your advisors determine that you should incorporate or form a partnership, do so within 30 days.

❏ Put your own home in a trust and record it at the courthouse. Advise your insurance company, mortgage company, and tax assessor.

❏ Check with your insurance company to see if you need to change the titling or type of your insurance policy as you begin a successful real estate business.

❏ Keep looking for and finding deals. Flip them, keep them, lease-option them, rent them out! Prosper and have fun. (Please e-mail me your name and address so you can be put on my mailing list.)

Make and review your action plan for each day, week, month, and year. Plan well, and you'll do well!

Set Up a Prospecting System

One deal is great, but it will take many deals to make a fortune. Set high marketing goals to ensure a perpetual stream of prospects. For example, you might resolve that every week you will

- run two to three ads to locate properties.
- send out 100 letters to locate properties.
- send out letters to 100 potential investors, 100 real estate agents, 100 nonprofit organizations, 100 FSBO properties, 100 contractors, 50 loan officers, and so forth.
- follow up on the previous week's letters with a telemarketing campaign. When you're starting out, place the calls yourself. Later, you can hire a telemarketing firm to fill out fact sheets on potential prospects for you to pursue. Even basic telemarketing works like crazy, and when coupled with direct mail can increase your response rate up to 400 percent.
- approach ten people with offers.

As you experiment with marketing and promotional activities, you will learn which work best for you. If you repeat them weekly, you will have an ongoing, efficient system in place that's operating and working for you every single day of the week.

Develop and maintain a list of property investors and buyers. Make sure the database includes their names, addresses, phone numbers, fax numbers, e-mail addresses, and what kind of property they prefer to buy. You can save time and look very professional by maintaining this information in a contact-management program that lets you mail, phone, or e-mail prospects with the touch of a computer button.

Stay in regular contact with these people. Check to see what buyers are looking for. Follow up on sellers to see if they are ready to deal, have lowered a price, or have another property for sale. Be persistent. If I need to talk to prospects I will call them every day, sometimes twice a day, until we talk.

Be Patient—and Don't Be Afraid to Lose

Some deals may take months, or even years. People who won't sell or buy now may do so later. Keep track of everyone and everything for at least four years. Review old files and possible investments every few months. Make those phone calls and visits again. I have bought houses that I first looked at three years earlier. It took that long for the sellers to come around or for their circumstances to change.

Be nice to everyone, regardless of position. Two of my best deals came from a down-and-out janitor I met cleaning a convention center. Because I was friendly toward him, I was able to buy two houses from him. I helped save him thousands of dollars he would have lost from a foreclosure, and kept him from becoming homeless. And he helped me make thousands of dollars on the good deals.

Be patient. Wait for the really good deals. If one slips by or you lose a few, don't worry. If you don't lose on a deal every now and then, you are probably not doing enough deals. I have lost some money before, but I learned a great lesson: Another, better deal will always come along.

Organize Your Papers

Most investors have information scattered all around the office. They've got files by the coffee pot, telephone slips near the door, and yellow stickies under their car seat!

Handling multiple deals is complex, and it is best to be organized from the beginning. Get a daily calendar. Write things down. Keep good notes. Set up neatly labeled files you can consult at will. My files consist of the following:

- Investment possibilities
- A file for each property with all documents and notes—including comparables, appraisals, lists, and prices of repairs, receipts, insurance, and tax information
- A hot sheet list of potential investment (wholesale) buyers and retail buyers with their names, addresses, preferences, and phone and fax numbers. I constantly update and add to this list.
- A "To Do Today" file

- A list of all my contractors, repair people, insurance agents, and attorneys
- Tenant files, which are constantly updated

Don't just keep files for deals in progress. Keep a file on every property you look at, are considering, or own. Don't throw away files on properties you've sold. You may need them in the future.

Take before-and-after pictures of every property that you buy or flip and keep them in the file or in a separate photo album to track your business.

Get a separate business phone line, answering machine, or answering service. Return all phone calls within four hours and always respond to all calls the same day you receive them. Even if you cannot talk, acknowledge the call. This will put you ahead of 95 percent of your competition. I find good deals because I am usually the first to call.

Also, it is always a good idea to carry with you a file with contracts and leases ready to be signed. You never know when they'll come in handy.

Set Up Bookkeeping and Recordkeeping Systems

Have someone help you set up an easy-to-use bookkeeping system. An inexpensive software program like Quicken and Microsoft Money can easily be adapted for real estate.

But you don't need to keep your books on a computer. I know plenty of people who still track expenses and income in ledger books. You don't even have to keep your own books! I let my accountant do all my bookkeeping and bill paying. At year's end, he has all the records he needs for taxes; meanwhile, I don't have to worry about paperwork so I can concentrate on doing deals. Financial paperwork isn't a strength for many entrepreneurs, so why not let a professional do it? One extra deal a month more than pays for his time and I have clean, professional ledgers and records.

Set up a separate banking account for your real estate expenses. Keep all checks and receipts. Be able to account for everything when tax season arrives. You will be able to write off a lot of expenses: business travel and meals, office supplies, a possible home office, and a car driven for business purposes (keep a log of miles).

R O B E R T ' S   R U L E S

Here are my rules for success:

- Set your goals. Plan how to get there, and go for it.

- Eat right and exercise. Try not to eat anything artificial. Exercise for 30 minutes to an hour, three or four times a week. It is great for the body and the mind. It should be your time, your break.

- Always learn. Take classes. Get more degrees. Go to seminars and speeches. I learn new things all of the time. Talk to older people who have done what you are doing and learn from their successes and mistakes.

- Share your experiences with a relative, a loved one, or a friend. It is a lot more fun to ride around and look at properties *with* someone.

- Perform a random act of kindness daily—be extra polite; help someone with a package; make an elderly person smile; give an unexpected gift.

- Be sure to take a break every now and then.

- Have fun. If it's not enjoyable, don't do it.

- Enjoy the infinite rewards.

Analyzing a Property

Use the worksheets in this appendix to analyze a property and determine whether it's truly a "good deal." Feel free to use or copy any of them. However, consult your attorney and/or accountant before relying on these documents or any of the information contained in them.

Property Information Worksheet
Home Inspection Checklist
Rehab Worksheet
Property Acquisition Worksheet

Property Information Worksheet

Property Address   Referred by:

City   State   Zip

Map/Parcel   Legal   Trust Deed Book Page   Deed Book/Page

Current Owner   Phone   Spouse

Date Purchased

Purchase Price

Mortgage Amount   Interest Rate   %

Years Amortized   P&I Last Payment Made   Approximate Balance

# of Elapsed Payments

Amount Needed to Reinstate   Payoff Amount

Mortgage Co.   Contact   Phone

Foreclosure Date   Trustee   Phone

2nd Mortgage Held By

Contact   Phone

Amount   Int. Rate   %   Date Originated   Book Page

Approximate Balance   Account #   Trustee   Ph. #

3rd Mortgage Held By

Contact   Phone

Amount   Int. Rate   %   Date Originated   Book Page

Approximate Balance   Account #   Trustee   Ph. #

Lien: Amount $ Date   Book/Page

Metro Liens: Amount $ Date   Book/Page

IRS Liens: Amount $ Date   Book/Page

Contact   Phone

State Tax Liens: Amount $ Date   Book/Page

Contact   Phone

Bankruptcy: Chapter   Date Filed   Case#   SS#

Attorney Phone   Date Discharged/Dismissed

Relief from Automatic Stay Granted

Neighbor Phone   Neighbor Phone

Other Family Member(s) Phone

NOTES:

Home Inspection Checklist

Examine Exterior of Home

1. Foundation:
   - ❏ Type
   - ❏ Condition *(missing mortar in joints, open holes, cracks, other damage)*
   - ❏ Comments:

2. Roof:
   - ❏ Type
   - ❏ Shingles *(missing pieces, cracking, damage)*
   - ❏ Framing *(bowed sheathing, sagging ridge)*
   - ❏ Comments:

3. Windows:
   - ❏ Type
   - ❏ Condition *(caulking needed, broken glass, missing putty, missing latches)*
   - ❏ Comments:

4. Chimney:
   - ❏ Condition *(missing mortar, damaged bricks, crumbling or cracking brickwork)*
   - ❏ Flashing *(cemented over, open gaps or holes, needs overall repair)*
   - ❏ Comments:

5. Trim:
   - ❏ Condition *(decaying wood, missing sections, peeling or chipped paint)*
   - ❏ Comments:

6. Gutters:
   - ❏ Type
   - ❏ Condition *(leaking, decaying, damaged, cracked)*
   - ❏ Comments:

7. Siding:
   - ❏ Type
   - ❏ Condition *(decaying, cracked, dented, damaged)*
   - ❏ Repairs required *(peeling paint, rusting, replace or repair missing sections)*
   - ❏ Comments:

Home Inspection Checklist (Continued)

Examine Exterior of Home (Continued)

8. Downspouts:
   - ❏ Type
   - ❏ Condition *(open seams, missing sections, rusting)*
   - ❏ Discharging to foundation (yes/no)
   - ❏ Comments:

9. Roof Vents:
   - ❏ Flashing *(defective, needs repair, leaking)*
   - ❏ Condition *(broken, damaged, missing)*
   - ❏ Comments:

10. Entrances:
    - ❏ Condition of doors *(fair, good, needs repair)*
    - ❏ Condition of steps *(decaying, deteriorating brickwork, unsafe for use)*
    - ❏ Rails (yes/no)
    - ❏ Comments:

11. Foundation Windows:
    - ❏ Type
    - ❏ Condition *(decaying, rusting, broken)*
    - ❏ Comments:

12. Porches:
    - ❏ Location
    - ❏ Condition *(decaying or damaged wood, sips of wood-boring insects, needs repair)*
    - ❏ Comments:

13. Skylights:
    - ❏ Damage *(missing putty, cracked glass, decaying or damaged frame)*
    - ❏ Comments:

14. Garage:
    - ❏ Attached/Detached
    - ❏ Condition *(needs repair and winterizing)*
    - ❏ Comments:

Home Inspection Checklist (Continued)

Examine Exterior of Home (Continued)

15. Driveway:
    - ❏ Condition (*cracking, decaying, heaving; needs repair—minor, major*)
    - ❏ Comments:

16. Low Wood Members:
    - ❏ Location _____
    - ❏ Condition (*decaying, insect activity, needs replacement*)
    - ❏ Comments:

17. Grade:
    - ❏ Does surface water flow toward house/building? (location _____)
    - ❏ Drywalls (yes/no)
    - ❏ Possibility of flooding (yes/no)
    - ❏ Comments:

18. Energy Losses:
    - ❏ Location(s) _____
    - ❏ Type(s) (*open gaps in siding, loose or missing trim, trim needs caulking, weather-stripping needed around windows and doors*)
    - ❏ Comments:

19. Landscaping:
    - ❏ Overgrown shrubs (yes/no)
    - ❏ Ivy on house (yes/no)
    - ❏ Overhanging tree branches (yes/no)
    - ❏ Location _____
    - ❏ Comments:

20. Fences:
    - ❏ Types
    - ❏ Condition (*rusting, decaying*)
    - ❏ Comments:

Home Inspection Checklist (Continued)

Examine Exterior of Home (Continued)

21. Retaining Wall:
    - ❑ Type
    - ❑ Weep holes (yes/no)
    - ❑ Condition *(decaying, needs repair)*
    - ❑ Comments:

22. Paths:
    - ❑ Condition *(settled, unsafe to use, cracked, damaged)*
    - ❑ Comments:

23. Structural Pests:
    - ❑ Signs of *(carpenter ants, termites, cockroaches, powder-post beetles)*
    - ❑ Location of damage _____
    - ❑ Comments:

Mechanical Systems

1. Heating:
    - ❑ Type
    - ❑ Condition *(functions, needs repairs)*
    - ❑ Type of fuel used *(oil, gas)*
    - ❑ Fire-stopping needed (yes/no)
    - ❑ Safety valves and shut-offs work properly (yes/no)
    - ❑ Sufficient heat is produced (yes/no) Zones (1/2/3)
    - ❑ Needs servicing or cleaning (yes/no)

2. Plumbing:
    - ❑ Drainage *(poor, fair, good)*
    - ❑ Water pressure *(adequate, inadequate)*
    - ❑ Leaks (yes/no)
    - ❑ Septic or cesspool system works properly (yes/no)
    - ❑ Use of lead waterlines or lead traps (yes/no)
    - ❑ Sufficient amount of shut-off valves (yes/no)
    - ❑ Working (yes/no)

Home Inspection Checklist (Continued)

Mechanical Systems (Continued)

3. Domestic Hot Water:
   - ❏ Type
   - ❏ Condition of tank *(leaking, corrosion, needs replacement)*
   - ❏ Type of fuel *(electricity, oil, gas)*
   - ❏ Safety valves working (yes/no)
   - ❏ Size of tank
   - ❏ Sufficient hot water (yes/no)
   - ❏ Location _____

4. Electrical:
   - ❏ How many amps (60, 100, 150, 200)
   - ❏ Main disconnect working (yes/no)
   - ❏ Serviced grounded (yes/no)
   - ❏ Use of *(lamp cord, knob and tube wiring)*
   - ❏ Aluminum wiring (yes/no)
   - ❏ Ground fault interrupters (yes/no)

5. Solar:
   - ❏ Type *(active or passive, heat or hot water)*
   - ❏ Working (yes/no)
   - ❏ Fully insulated (yes/no)
   - ❏ Condition of pipes
   - ❏ Solar collector location _____

6. Air Conditioner:
   - ❏ Condition *(good, fair, needs repair)*
   - ❏ Size of unit
   - ❏ Type *(split, integral)*
   - ❏ Last servicing

Basement Interior

1. Water Penetration:
   - ❏ Location
   - ❏ Efflorescence (yes/no)
   - ❏ Sump pump working (yes/no)
   - ❏ Comments:

Home Inspection Checklist (Continued)

Basement Interior (Continued)

2. Cellar Floor:
   ❏ Condition *(holes, evidence of water, cracks, needs repair)*
   ❏ Comments:

3. Foundation Walls:
   ❏ Accessible/Inaccessible
   ❏ Condition *(poor, fair, good)*
   ❏ Comments:

4. Main Girder:
   ❏ Condition *(resting on foundation, needs repair)*
   ❏ Evidence of deterioration, decay, or insect activity (yes/no) Extent:
   ❏ Comments:

5. Insect Activity:
   ❏ Type
   ❏ Extent of damage
   ❏ Location _____
   ❏ Comments:

6. Floor Joists:
   ❏ Condition *(damaged, decaying, rotting, sagging)*
   ❏ Comments:

7. Posts:
   ❏ Type
   ❏ Condition *(fair, good, need repairs)*
   ❏ Comments:

8. Insulation:
   ❏ Type
   ❏ Condition
   ❏ Location _____
   ❏ Amount of insulation
   ❏ Vapor barrier (yes/no)
   ❏ Comments:

Home Inspection Checklist (Continued)

Basement Interior (Continued)

9. Crawl Spaces: (yes/no)
   - ❏ Condition
   - ❏ Location _____
   - ❏ Comments:

The Attic

1. Insulation:
   - ❏ Type
   - ❏ Amount
   - ❏ Location _____
   - ❏ Condition (*damaged, needs to be replaced*)
   - ❏ Comments:

2. Leaks:
   - ❏ Around the chimney (yes/no)
   - ❏ Vent pipe leaks (yes/no)
   - ❏ Daylight visible from attic (yes/no)
   - ❏ Location _____
   - ❏ Comments:

3. Ventilation:
   - ❏ Kind (*gable, roof, ridge, soffit*)
   - ❏ Needs repairs (yes/no)
   - ❏ Sufficient ventilation (yes/no)
   - ❏ Sips of condensation (yes/no)
   - ❏ Comments:

4. Improper Venting into Attic:
   - ❏ Location (*bathroom vents, kitchen vents*) _____
   - ❏ Comments:

5. Framing:
   - ❏ Condition (*structurally sound, insect activity, decaying*)
   - ❏ Comments:

Home Inspection Checklist (Continued)

Kitchen

1. Stove:
   - ❏ Type of fuel *(electricity, gas, oil)*
   - ❏ Unit working (yes/no)
   - ❏ Comments:

2. Sink:
   - ❏ Condition *(poor, fair, good)*
   - ❏ Piping *(damaged, leaks, needs replacement)*
   - ❏ Comments:

3. Ceilings:
   - ❏ Condition
   - ❏ Comments:

4. Appliances:
   - ❏ Types
   - ❏ Ages
   - ❏ Condition
   - ❏ Working (yes/no)
   - ❏ Comments:

5. Walls:
   - ❏ Need repairs (yes/no)
   - ❏ Location _____
   - ❏ Comments:

6. Floors:
   - ❏ Needs replacement (yes/no)
   - ❏ Comments:

7. Ventilation and Light:
   - ❏ Adequate/Inadequate
   - ❏ Comments:

8. Heat:
   - ❏ Yes/No
   - ❏ Comments:

Home Inspection Checklist (Continued)

Kitchen (Continued)

9. Cabinets and Counter Space:
   ❑ Adequate/Inadequate
   ❑ Comments:

10. Electrical Outlets:
   ❑ Sufficient/Need more outlets
   ❑ Comments:

Bathrooms

1. Fixtures:
   ❑ Condition *(poor, fair, good)*
   ❑ Leaks (yes/no)
   ❑ Damaged or chipped fixtures (yes/no) Location _____
   ❑ Faucets dripping (yes/no)
   ❑ Comments:

2. Ventilation:
   ❑ Type *(mechanical vents, windows)*
   ❑ Comments:

3. Ceilings:
   ❑ In need of repairs (yes/no)
   ❑ Comments:

4. Ground Fault Interrupter:
   ❑ Yes/No
   ❑ Working (yes/no)
   ❑ Comments:

5. Water Pressure:
   ❑ Adequate/Needs repairs
   ❑ Comments:

6. Tile:
   ❑ Condition *(missing, chipped, broken, falling off of walls)*
   ❑ Comments:

Home Inspection Checklist (Continued)

Bathrooms (Continued)

7. Heat:
   - ❑ Yes/No
   - ❑ Comments:

8. Floors:
   - ❑ Condition (*tile pulling up, needs replacement, deteriorating or decaying*)
   - ❑ Comments:

9. Walls:
   - ❑ Condition (*damaged walls from water, needs repair, loose plaster*)
   - ❑ Location for repairs _____
   - ❑ Comments:

10. Drainage:
   - ❑ Normal/Sluggish
   - ❑ Comments:

Rooms

1. Walls:
   - ❑ Condition (*needs repair, missing sections, holes*)
   - ❑ Location for repairs _____
   - ❑ Comments:

2. Windows:
   - ❑ New storm windows needed?
   - ❑ Condition (*need repairs, general tightening up*)
   - ❑ Comments:

3. Heating:
   - ❑ Register/Rradiator/None
   - ❑ Comments:

4. Closets:
   - ❑ Sufficient size/Insufficient size
   - ❑ Need more closets or closet space
   - ❑ Comments:

5. Ceilings:
   - ❑ Condition (*sagging plaster, water stains, cracks, damaged areas*)
   - ❑ Comments:

Home Inspection Checklist (Continued)

Rooms (Continued)

6. Floors:
   - ❏ Condition *(refinish, install new floor, replace carpeting)*
   - ❏ Comments:

7. Doors:
   - ❏ Condition *(damaged, needs repair, missing)*
   - ❏ Comments:

8. Electrical:
   - ❏ Overhead lights/Need additional outlets
   - ❏ Comments:

9. Other:

Fireplace and/or Stove

1. Safety Hazards:
   - ❏ Location _____
   - ❏ Types
   - ❏ Comments:

2. Condition of Flue Pipe:
   - ❏ Poor/Fair/Good/Needs replacement
   - ❏ Comments:

3. Needs Cleaning:
   - ❏ Yes/No
   - ❏ Last cleaning/Servicing date
   - ❏ Comments:

4. Permit for Stove:
   - ❏ Yes/No
   - ❏ Comments:

5. Proximity to Combustible Materials:
   - ❏ Location _____
   - ❏ Comments:

Rehab Worksheet

CASH OUT OF POCKET:

    Down Payment   _____

    Closing Costs   _____

    Appraisal   _____

    Termite letter   _____

    Survey   _____

    Title Insurance   _____

    Miscellaneous   _____

                                  1. **Total** _____

COST OF REHAB: _____

    Flooring   _____

    Painting   _____

    Roofing   _____

    Windows/Screens   _____

    Kitchen (faucets, cabinets, etc.)   _____

    Bathroom(s) (vanity, sink, tub, etc.) _____

    Bedroom(s)   _____

    Decorations (ceiling fans, brass, etc.) _____

    Doors   _____

    Foundation   _____

    Fireplace(s)   _____

    Locks   _____

    Plumbing   _____

    Insulation   _____

                                  2. **Total** _____

    Total multiplied by a 15% repair cost overrun _____

ESTIMATED HOLDING COSTS:

    # Months × Mortgage _____ + Insurance _____ + Taxes _____ + Utilities _____

                                  3. **Total** _____

Rehab Worksheet (Continued)

ESTIMATED SELLING COSTS (following rehab):

Closing Costs _____

Attorney fees _____

Document/Transfer taxes _____

Commissions _____

4. **Total** _____

Total estimated acquisition, rehab & selling costs

Add totals from lines 1, 2, 3, and 4   5. _____

Plus (+) Mortgage Balance Payoff   5a. _____

Total cost of property (Add lines 5 and 5a)   6. _____

Total projected selling price (following rehab)   7. _____

Total profit (Subtract Line 6 from Line 7)   _____

Property Acquisition Worksheet

ADDRESS:

Estimated Sales Price after Fix-Up $

Down Payment
Closing Costs
Commission
Appraisal
Termite
Miscellaneous

= Total Expense to Buy

Rehab Budget
Cost Overruns (+/–15%)

= Total Rehab Costs

Payments for _____ Months
Property Tax
Insurance

= Total Holding Costs

(+ your time and cost of your capital)

Sale Closing Costs
Commission
Advertising, Telemarketing

= Total Sales Costs

$ Mortgage Payoffs

Total Sales Price
Expense to Buy
Total Rehab Costs
Total Holding Costs
Total Sales Costs

= Your Profit

Financial Forms

Use these forms to determine whether you qualify for conventional financing, and to prepare a financing package for your banker. Feel free to use or copy any of them. However, consult your attorney and/or accountant before relying on these documents or any of the information contained in them.

Loan Qualification Worksheet
Sample Loan Request
Sample Project Description: Greenwood Court Project
Description of Other Real Estate Owned

Loan Qualification Worksheet

The following worksheet will allow you to calculate the mortgage loan amount for which you qualify.

MAXIMUM DEBT ALLOWED

Stable Monthly Income	$ _____
(Multiply by 28)	× 28%
Maximum Monthly Housing Expense	= $ _____
Stable Monthly Income	$ _____
(Multiply by 36)	× 36%
Maximum Monthly Housing Expense	
Plus Other Obligations	= $ _____

ACTUAL AND ANTICIPATED EXPENSES

Monthly Housing Expense		Total Monthly Expenses	
Principal + Interest	$ _____	Total Housing	$ _____
Red Estate Taxes	$ _____	Installment Debt	$ _____
Insurance Premium	$ _____	Revolving Charges	$ _____
Homeowners Assoc.	$ _____	Alimony, etc.	$ _____
Other	$ _____		
Total	$ _____	Total	$ _____

Compare actual to maximum expenses allowed. Actual expenses should not exceed the maximum allowed.

These qualifications are the standard current guidelines used by most lenders in your area.

Sample Loan Request

Loan Request

1804 Fatherland Street—4 bedroom, 1½ bath, Historic Edgefield

This is a completely renovated historic home in Edgefield. It has hardwood floors, large rooms, a deck, high ceilings. Everything in the house has been completely redone. Next door, on one side, lives the assistant symphony conductor who paid over $100,000 for her home. On the other side is a 2-bedroom house that is listed for $82,000. 1 have a contract on the house to lease/purchase it for $78,000; $800/month rent.

> Appraisal Value = $75,000-$85,000
> Gross Rent = $800/month
> Vacancy and Repairs = $50/month
> Lease/Purchase
> Taxes and Insurance = $69/month
> Net Rent = $681/month

1st Mortgage Payment = $507/month
($50,000 loan, 9%, 180 months)

Property has no debt on it.

Greenwood Court Project

Brief Description

Sixteen brick duplexes each containing two 2-bedroom, 1-bath apartments of about 850 square feet, located in a nice area of West Nashville. All but about 8 units are rented for between $353 to $400 a month. Over 90 percent of the tenants are in the Section 8 program, which means the government pays all or most of the rent. All of the tenants and rents qualify as low or very low income according to the Department of Housing and Urban Development (HUD).

The vacancies are due to the fact that they are the last ones to be rehabilitated. All of the other units have just gone through a major rehabilitation. The units are located in a dead-end court, which enables the owner to control the area.

Long-Term Plan

To rent the majority of the units to Section 8 tenants. Some of the units may be converted to 3 bedrooms to increase the rents to about $450 a side as opposed to $375 a side. The cost to do this is about $1,000 a unit. Though demand for 2-bedroom units is high, the demand for 3-bedroom units is incredibly high.

The Section 8 Program

This program is for low-income families mainly headed by single mothers with children. The money is allotted for 10 years, for each certificate holder or tenant, by HUD and administered by MDHA.

The leases are guaranteed for a year. Usually, the government pays all of the rent. Sometimes the tenant has to pay a small amount. MDHA inspects the units twice a year and requires them to be in good repair.

Section 8 and MDHA. also insure against damages for up to 2 months' rent, or about $750 for each unit. If the tenant damages the unit, the landlord can collect the damage money from Section 8.

The demand for Section 8 housing is extremely high. The quantity and quality of housing available for Section 8 tenants is very low. Thus, I have been operating my 20 duplexes at a 100 percent occupancy rate with waiting lists for each property. The landlord can screen the tenants and does not have to rent to someone he or she does not want to rent to.

Greenwood Court Project (Continued)

Financial Details

Per building purchase price	$39,000.00
18% down payment	7,020.00
Amount financed	31,980.00
Monthly payment, 15 years @ 8.5% interest	314.92.00
Taxes per month	40.00
Insurance per month	25.00
Monthly payment w/taxes and insurance	379.92.00
Current rent per duplex	750.00
Free cash flow per month	370.08

Risks

Vacancy and repair risks are inherent in real estate. The vacancy risk should be about 0. Again, the demand for Section 8 housing is high. I have not advertised in almost a year and have kept my 20 duplexes full. I get about 10 to 20 calls a week from people looking for housing. Furthermore, the Greenwood Project is in an excellent location. The repair costs are also minimal because Section 8 guarantees about two months' rent for damage repair. That is about $750 per unit. All of my appliances are insured, so it is very difficult for a tenant to do more than $750 worth of damage, especially if they are managed properly. Also, only one side of each duplex has to stay rented in order to pay the note, taxes, and insurance.

Management

I personally manage all of my properties. I walk through each unit at least once every 30 days. I have provided and intend to continue providing the highest quality low- and moderate-income housing in Davidson County. All of my units are like new when the tenants move in, and I try to keep them that way.

I use licensed, bonded contractors for all of my repairs. They work for about $7 an hour and do quality work. Thus, whatever repairs I do incur are handled promptly, professionally, and reasonably.

Real Estate Schedule For Robert Shemin Date: 10-01-99	Duplexes 1 4656-4658 Forest Ridge	2 4625-4627 Forest Ridge	3 4653-4655 Forest Ridge	4 2300-2302 Campbell
Title	Robert Shemin	Robert Shemin	Robert Shemin	Robert Shemin
Purchase Price	$39,000	$ 38,700	$48,000	$47,500
Year Purchased	1991	1991	1991	1991
Appraised Value	$50,000	$ 49,000	$53,000	$54,000
Debt	$34,000	$ 33,900	$38,450	$39,000
Mortgage Holder	Kislak	Kislak	Kislak	Kislak
Monthly Payment Taxes and Insurance Included	$ 428	$ 404	$ 450	$ 422
Gross Monthly Rent	$ 740	$ 739	$ 730	$ 750
Gross Monthly Income	$ 312	$ 335	$ 280	$ 328
Total Free Cash Flow		$ 6,767		
Vacancy & Repairs Expenses 90% of leases are Section 8, which are guaranteed for a year.		$ 1,200		
Monthly Income		$ 5,567		
Total Equity		$362,862		

Description of Other Real Estate Owned

(All Duplexes)

PROPERTY 1

4656-58 FORREST RIDGE DRIVE
HERMITAGE, TENNESSEE

GROSS RENT	$730
MINUS PAYMENT	372
MINUS TAXES AND INSURANCE	
FREE CASH FLOW	$358/MONTH
TOTAL INVESTMENT	$10,917

PROPERTY 2

2716 C-D EASTLAND

GROSS RENT	$830
MINUS PAYMENT	
MINUS TAXES AND INSURANCE	493
FREE CASH FLOW	$337/MONTH
TOTAL INVESTMENT	$10,936

APPENDIX C

Contracts, Deeds, and Other Legal Forms

This appendix contains samples of the many forms you will use as you negotiate for, control, and hold real estate. Feel free to use or copy any of them. However, consult your attorney and/or accountant before relying on these documents or any of the information contained in them.

Contract of Sale
Contract to Purchase Real Estate
Option to Purchase Real Estate
Option to Purchase Real Estate
Agreement for Deed
Land Trust
Land Installment Contract
Promissory Note
Quitclaim Deed
Warranty Deed to Trustee
Disclosure Form
Sample Notice of Foreclosure

CONTRACT OF SALE

THIS CONTRACT of sale made this_____ day of _____ 200____, by and between _____ hereinafter called SELLER and_____ hereinafter called BUYER.

WITNESSETH: That the seller in considerations of the sum of _____ Dollars as earnest money and in part payment of the purchase price has this day sold and does hereby agree to convey by a good and valid warranty deed to said buyer, or to such person as he may in writing direct the following described real estate in _____ County, Tennessee, to wit:

CONSIDERATION: Buyer agrees to purchase said real estate and to pay therefor the sum of _____ Dollars, upon the following terms: $ _____ cash, balance.

MISCELLANEOUS CONDITIONS:

TITLE INSURANCE: The _____ or his agent, at seller's expense, agrees to make application to the _____ for Title Insurance on the above property and if after examination by this Company the title is found insurable the buyer hereby agrees to accept a title Policy issued by said Company in it's usual form and to comply with this contract. WITHIN TEN DAYS after receiving a report on the title, and it is agreed that such report shall be conclusive evidence of good title subject to the exceptions therein stated, otherwise that the earnest money is to be refunded.

Should the buyer default in the performance of this contract on his part at the time and in the manner specified then at seller's option the earnest money shall be forfeited as liquidated damages. But such forfeiture shall not prevent suit for the specific performance of this contract.

In the event of default in the terms of this contract for any reason on the part of the seller and in the event it becomes necessary, due to any fault of the sellers that the earnest money herein above shown, must be returned to the buyer, then the seller shall be liable to the agent herein for the full commission set out in this contract.

The words SELLER and BUYER when used in this contract shall be construed as plural whenever the number of parties to this contract so requires.

SELLER ACKNOWLEDGEMENT: Seller acknowledges that buyer is a licensed Real Estate Broker and is purchasing said property for rental or resale.

ADJUSTMENTS TO BE MADE AT TIME OF CLOSING:

    (1) Sellers Escrow Deposits to be _____

    (2) Taxes for Current Year _____

    (3) Sellers Fire Insurance to be _____

    (4) Existing Leases or Rents _____

Possession to be _____

Conveyance to be subject to existing Building Restrictions and/or Zoning Ordinances
_____ Seller to bear risk of hazard loss to date of deed.

Purchaser: _____   Seller: _____

Purchaser: _____   Seller: _____

Deed Property to: _____

CONTRACT TO PURCHASE REAL ESTATE

1. I/We offer to purchase from Seller the following described real estate, together with all improvements thereon and all appurtenant rights, located at:

   Address: _____ City: _____

   County: _____ State: _____ Zip: _____

2. The purchase price is to be $ _____ payable as follows:

3. The conditions of the Purchase are as follows:
   a. Subject to review, inspection, and written approval of my financial partner.
   b. Purchaser shall have the right to assign his/her interest in this contract prior to escrow.
   c. Seller agrees to allow purchaser to show property to prospective partners and clients prior to closing.

4. Is there an Addendum to this contract ? YES _____ NO_____

5. Is this deal "All Cash" or "Terms"? "All Cash"_____ "Terms" _____

6. Possession is to be given on or before _____ .

7. Seller agrees to pay all Taxes and Assessments up to and including the month of _____ , 200____ .

8. Closing costs shall be paid by: Seller _____ Purchaser _____ Split _____

9. Closing date shall be on or before _____, 200___, with title to the above described real estate to be conveyed by Warranty Deed with release of dower. Title is to be free, clear, and unencumbered, free of building orders, subject to zoning regulations of record, and except easements and restrictions of record, and except.

10. This offer, when accepted, comprises the entire agreement of Purchaser and Seller, and it is agreed that no other representation or agreements have been made or relied upon.

11. This offer is to remain open for acceptance until _____ .

Date: _____ Date: _____

Seller _____ Purchaser _____

Seller _____ Purchaser _____

OPTION TO PURCHASE REAL ESTATE

This Agreement, made this _____ day of _____, 200___, by and between _____ (the "Optioner") and _____ ("Optionee"), for and in consideration of the sum of dollars ($) ("Option Fee") paid by Optionee to Optioner, the receipt of which is hereby acknowledged, the Optioner hereby gives and grants unto the Optionee, his/her heirs, representatives and assigns, the right of purchasing, on or before the _____ day of _____ 200____, (the "Option Date") the following described real estate situated in _____ County, (State), to wit: _____ (the "Property") for the total purchase price of _____ Dollars ($_____) ("Purchase Price"). If the Optionee shall so elect to purchase the Property pursuant to this Agreement, the Optionee shall notify the Optioner in writing ("Notice of Election") at _____ on or before the Option Date.

If Optionee provides Optioner with a Notice of Election, the Optionee, prior to the Option Date shall deliver to Optioner a contract for the sale of the Property to Optionee and the Optioner shall agree to convey the Property to Optionee, his/her heirs, representatives or assigns, by warranty deed, free and clear of all liens, encumbrances, or taxes to the date of closing of the purchase. Optioner further agrees, that within 30 days after receipt of the Notice of Election, Optioner shall deliver to Optionee a policy of title insurance in the full sum of the Purchase Price showing full and merchantable title to said real estate. On the date of closing (to be mutually agreed on by the parties hereto), Optionee, his/her heirs, representatives, or assigns shall deliver to Optioner the full Purchase Price.

If the Optionee does not exercise the option hereunder, or fails to fully perform the conditions herein within the time stated, this Agreement shall terminate and the Option Fee paid by Optionee shall be retained by Optioner.

In the event that this Agreement is terminated by reason of failure to perform under the terms hereunder, either party may institute a cause of action in law or equity and the party deemed to be at fault shall pay all reasonable attorney fees and expenses of the other party.

This Agreement constitutes the entire agreement of the parties hereto and may not be modified except by a written document signed by all parties.

IN WITNESS HEREOF, the parties have executed this Agreement the day and year first above written.

Optioner   Optionee

OPTION TO PURCHASE REAL ESTATE

This agreement, made this _____ day of _____, 200___, by and between _____, hereinafter called Optioner, and _____, hereinafter called Optionee, Witnesseth, that for and in consideration of the sum of:

_____ Dollars ($_____) paid by Optionee to Optioner, the receipt whereof is hereby acknowledge the Optioner hereby gives and grants unto the Optionee heirs, personal representatives, and assigns, the right of purchasing, on or before the _____ day of _____, 200___, the following described real estate situated in _____ County (State) to wit:

_____ for the total purchase price of _____ Dollars ($_____). Shall be paid as follows: _____
_____.

If the Optionee elects to purchase the said real estate pursuant to this Option, Optionee shall give notice to such Optioner, at _____, on or before the _____ day of _____, 209_____.

If the Optionee shall so elect to purchase said real estate, and shall give of such election as herein provided within the time required, and shall tender the required amount of cash and a real estate contract or other security to Optioner, on the real estate hereinabove particularly described, then Optioner agrees to convey the real estate to Optionee heirs or assigns, by warranty deed, free and clear of all liens, encumbrances, and taxes, to the date of closing of the purchase. Optioner further agrees that on such election by Optionee, to deliver to Optionee, within 30 days after receipt of such written notice of election to purchase, a policy of title insurance in the full sum of the purchase price showing merchantable title to said real estate.

If the Optionee does not exercise the privilege of purchase given and does not fully perform the conditions herein within the time herein stated, the privilege shall wholly cease and terminate and the sum of _____ Dollars ($_____), herein paid by Optionee shall be retained by Optioner.

If either party exercises the right to terminate this agreement for failure to perform or observe the obligations, agreements, or covenants of this agreement, the party at fault shall pay all reasonable attorney fees and expenses of the other party.

This agreement constitutes the entire agreement of the parties hereto and may not be modified except by a written document signed by all parties.

IN WITNESS WHEREOF, the parties have executed this the day and year first above written.

Optioner   Optionee

AGREEMENT FOR DEED

THIS AGREEMENT FOR DEED made this_____ day of _____ A.D., 200___, _____, BY AND BETWEEN _____ of the County of _____, State of _____, hereinafter referred to as SELLERS, and _____ hereinafter referred to as PURCHASERS.

WITNESSETH, That provided the said Purchasers shall first make the payments and perform the covenants hereinafter set forth on their part to be made and performed, the said Sellers covenant and agree to and will by good and sufficient warranty deed convey and assure to the said Purchasers, their heirs and assigns forever in fee simple, free and clear of all encumbrances, the following described land situated in _____ _____ County, _____ to wit:

The purchase price of said land is $_____ Dollars, of which the Purchasers have herewith paid to the Sellers the sum of $_____ Dollars and the Purchasers agree to pay to the Sellers the balance, to wit: the principal sum of $_____ Dollars, together with interest on so much of said principal sum as remains from time to time outstanding and unpaid at the rate of per centrum from _____ until paid; said principal and interest to be payable in payments consecutive on the _____ day of each and every month beginning with the _____ day of _____, 200___; said installments to be applied first to interest and balance to principal. If any payment is not received within _____ days of due date, there shall be a late charge of _____ % added. The Purchasers may prepay any part of the principal sum hereof in multiples of $_____ Dollars on any installment payment date, but any such prepayment shall not relieve the Purchasers from making the payment of the installment then due and any subsequent installment provided hereby unless at the time of such prepayment the Purchasers pay all sums unpaid hereon.

The Purchasers covenant and agree as follows: (a) to pay all taxes, fines, and assessments levied or assessed on said land subsequent to December 31, 200___, as and when the same respectively become due and shall exhibit to Sellers immediately after such payment the official receipts therefor; (b) to place and continuously keep on the building now or hereafter situate on said land fire and extended coverage insurance in the usual standard policy form in a sum not less than $_____ Dollars in such company or companies as may be approved by the Sellers and said policies shall be delivered up and held by the Sellers and contain the usual clauses making said policies payable to the Sellers as their interest may appear, and in the event any sum of money becomes payable under such policies, the Sellers shall have the right to receive and apply the sum on account of the indebtedness secured hereby; (c) to permit, commit, or suffer no waste, impairment, or deterioration of said property or any part thereof, (d) to at all times keep and maintain the buildings and improvements on said land in a good and tenantable state of repair and condition.

Time is of the essence in this agreement and in the event of any breach of this agreement or default on the part of the Purchasers of any kind whatsoever, the Sellers may without notice to the Purchasers exercise the following options: (a) to terminate this agreement and retain all sums of money theretofore paid by the Purchasers as liquidated damages and/or the reasonable rental value of said land, and to render said premises and take possession thereof fully and to all intents and purposes as if the Purchasers had no interest in said property whatsoever, or (b) to accelerate all sums of money secured by this agreement whether due by the literal terms hereof or not, and to foreclose this agreement in accordance with the rules of practice applicable to vendors' liens, in which event the Purchasers agree to pay all costs of collection and foreclosure, including reasonable attorney fee.

The words Seller, Sellers, Purchaser, and Purchasers, whether in the singular or plural as the case may be, wherever used herein shall be taken to mean and include the singular, if only one, and plural, jointly and severally, if more than one, and their respective heirs, assigns, and legal representatives; and that the word their taken to mean his, her, or its wherever the context hereof so implies or admits.

IN WITNESS WHEREOF, the parties hereto have hereunto set their hands and seals the day and year first above written.

_____   _____
Witness   SELLER

_____
Witness

_____   _____
Witness   PURCHASER

_____
Witness

STATE OF: _____
COUNTY OF: _____

Before me personally appeared _____ to me well known and known to me to be the person(s) described in and executed the foregoing instrument, and acknowledged to and before me that executed said instrument for the purpose therein expressed.

WITNESS my hand seal, and official seal this _____ day of _____, 200___.

Notary Public _____
State of _____
My Commission Expires: _____

STATE OF: _____
COUNTY OF: _____

Before me personally appeared _____ to me well known and known to me to be the person(s) described in and executed the foregoing instrument, and acknowledged to and before me that executed said instrument for the purpose therein expressed.

WITNESS my hand seal, and official seal this _____ day of _____, 200___.
Notary Public _____
State of _____
My Commission Expires: _____

This instrument was prepared by:

LAND TRUST

308 NEIL AVENUE TRUST

THIS AGREEMENT AND DECLARATION OF TRUST is made and entered into this _____ day of _____, 200___, by and between _____, as Grantors and Beneficiary, (hereinafter referred to as the "Beneficiary" or "Beneficiaries", whether one or more, which designation shall include all successors in interest of any beneficiary), and _____ whose address is _____ _____ (hereinafter referred to as the "Trustee", which designation shall include all successor trustees).

IT IS MUTUALLY AGREED AS FOLLOWS:

1. **Trust Property.** The Beneficiary is about to convey or cause to be conveyed to the Trustee by deed, absolute in form, the property described in the attached **Exhibit "A",** which said property shall be held by the Trustee, in trust, for the following uses and purposes, under the terms of this Agreement and shall be hereinafter referred to as the "Trust Property".
2. **Consideration.** No consideration has been paid by Trustee for such conveyance. The conveyance will be accepted and will be held by Trustee subject to all existing encumbrances, easements, restrictions, or other clouds or claims against the title thereto, whether the same are of record or otherwise. The property will be held on the trusts, terms, and conditions and for the purposes hereinafter set forth, until the whole of the trust estate is conveyed, free of this Trust, as hereinafter provided.
3. **Beneficiary.** The person(s) named in the attached **Exhibit "B"** are the Beneficiary(ies) of this Trust (referred to as "Beneficiary" or "Beneficiaries"), and as such, shall be entitled to all of the earnings, avails, and proceeds of the Trust Property according to their interests set opposite their respective names.
4. **Interests.** The interests of the Beneficiary shall consist solely of the following rights respecting the Trust Property:
   a. The right to direct the Trustee to convey or otherwise deal with the title to the Trust Property as hereinafter set out.
   b. The right to manage and control the Trust Property.
   c. The right to receive the proceeds and avails from the rental, sale, mortgage, or other disposition of the Trust Property.

The foregoing rights shall be deemed to be personal property and may be assigned and otherwise transferred as such. No beneficiary shall have any legal or equitable right, title, or interest as realty, in or to any real estate held in trust under this Agreement, or the right to require partition of that real estate, but shall have only the rights, as personally, set out above, and the death of a beneficiary shall not terminate this Trust or in any manner affect the powers of the Trustee.

5. **Power of Trustee.**

    a. With the consent of the Beneficiary, the Trustee shall have authority to issue notes or bonds and to secure the payment of the same by mortgaging the whole or any part of the Trust Property; to borrow money, giving notes therefor signed by him in his capacity as Trustee; to invest such part of the capital and the profits therefrom and the proceeds of the sale of bonds and notes in such real estate, equities in real estate, and mortgages in real estate in the United States of America, as he may deem advisable.

    b. With the consent of the Beneficiary, the Trustee shall have the authority to hold the legal title to all of the Trust Property, and shall have the exclusive management and control of the properly as if he were the absolute owner thereof, and the Trustee is hereby given full power to do all things and perform all acts that in his judgment are necessary and proper for the protection of the Trust Property and for the interest of the Beneficiary in the property of the Trust, subject to the restrictions, terms, and conditions herein set forth.

    c. Without prejudice to the general powers conferred on the Trustee hereunder, it is hereby declared that the Trustee shall have the following powers, with the consent of the Beneficiary:

        (1) To purchase any real property for the Trust at such times and on such terms as may seem advisable; to assume mortgages upon the property.

        (2) To sell at public auction or private sale, to barter, to exchange, or to otherwise dispose of any part, or the whole of the Trust Property that may from time to time form part of the Trust estate, subject to such restrictions and for such consideration for cash and/or for credit, and generally upon such terms and conditions as may seem judicious, to secure payment upon any loan or loans of the Trust, by mortgage with or without power of sale, and to include such provisions, terms, and conditions as may seem desirable.

        (3) To rent or lease the whole or any part of the Trust Property for long or short terms, but not for terms exceeding the term of the Trust then remaining.

        (4) To repair, alter, tear down, add to, or erect any building or buildings upon land belonging to the Trust; to fill, grade, drain, improve, and otherwise develop any land belonging to the Trust; to carry on, operate, or manage any building, apartment house, or hotel belonging to the Trust.

        (5) To make, execute, acknowledge, and deliver all deeds, releases, mortgages, leases, contracts, agreements, instruments, and other obligations of whatsoever nature relating to the Trust Property, and generally to have full power to do all things and perform all acts necessary to make the instruments proper and legal.

        (6) To collect notes, obligations, dividends, and all other payments that may be due and payable to the Trust; to deposit the proceeds thereof, as well as any other monies from whatsoever source they may be derived, in any suitable bank or depository, and to draw the same from time to time for the purposes herein provided.

(7) To pay all lawful taxes and assessments and the necessary expenses of the Trust, to employ such of officers, brokers, engineers, architects, carpenters, contractors, agents, counsel, and such other persons as may seem expedient, to designate their duties and fix their compensation; to fix a reasonable compensation for their own services to the Trust, as organizers thereof.

(8) To represent the Trust and the Beneficiary in all suits and legal proceedings relating to the Trust Property in any court of law of equity, or before any other bodies or tribunals; to begin suits and to prosecute them to final judgment or decree; to compromise claims or suits, and to submit the same to arbitration when, in their judgment, such course is necessary or proper.

(9) To arrange and pay for and keep in force in the name and for the benefit of the Trustee, such insurance as the Trustee may deem advisable, in such companies, in such amounts, and against such risks as determined necessary by the Trustee.

6. **Duties of Trustee.** It shall be the duty of the Trustee in addition to the other duties herein imposed upon him:

a. To keep a careful and complete record of all the beneficial interests in the Trust Property with the name and residence of the person or persons owning such beneficial interest, and such other items as they may deem of importance or as may be required by the Beneficiary.

b. To keep careful and accurate books showing the receipts and disbursements of the Trust and also of the Trust Property, and such other items as he may deem of importance or as the Beneficiary hereunder may require.

c. To keep books of the Trust open to the inspection of the Beneficiary at such reasonable times at the main office of the Trust as they may appoint.

d. To furnish the Beneficiary at special meetings, at which the same shall be requested, a careful, accurate, written report of their transactions as Trustees hereunder, of the financial standing of the Trust, and of such other information concerning the affairs of the Trust as they shall request.

e. To sell the Trust Property and distribute the proceeds therefrom:

(1) If any property shall remain in trust under this Agreement for a term that exceeds that allowed under applicable state law, the Trustee forthwith shall sell same at public sale after a reasonable public advertisement and reasonable notice to the Beneficiary and, after deducting its reasonable fees and expenses, the Trustee shall divide the proceeds of the sale among the then Beneficiaries as their interests may then appear, without any direction or consent whatsoever, or

(2) To transfer, set over, convey, and deliver to all the then Beneficiaries of this Trust their respective undivided interests in any nondivisible assets, or

(3) To transfer, set over, and deliver all of the assets of the Trust to its then Beneficiaries, in their respective proportionate shares, at any time when the assets of the Trust consist solely of cash.

7. **Compensation of Trustee.** The Beneficiary jointly and severally agrees that the Trustee shall receive reasonable compensation monthly for his services as Trustee hereunder.

8. **Liability of Trustee.** The Trustee and his successor as Trustee shall not be required to give a bond, and each Trustee shall be liable only for his own acts and then only as a result of his own gross negligence or bad faith.

9. **Removal of Trustee.** The Beneficiary shall have the power to remove a Trustee from his office or appoint a successor to succeed him.

10. **Resignation and Successor.**

    a. Any Trustee may resign his office with thirty (30) days' written notice to Beneficiary and Beneficiary shall proceed to elect a new Trustee to take the place of the Trustee who had resigned, but the resignation shall not take effect until a certificate thereof, signed, sealed, and acknowledged by the new Trustee and a certificate of the election of the new Trustee, signed and sworn to by the Beneficiary and containing an acceptance of the office, signed and acknowledged by the new Trustee, shall have been procured in a form that is acceptable for recording in the registries of deeds of all the counties in which properties held under this instrument are situated. If the Beneficiary shall fail to elect a new Trustee within thirty (30) days after the resignation, then the Trustee may petition any appropriate court in this state to accept his resignation and appoint a new Trustee.

    b. Any vacancy in the office of Trustee, whether arising from death or from any other cause not herein provided for, shall be filled within thirty (30) days from the date of the vacancy and the Beneficiary shall proceed to elect a new Trustee to fill the vacancy, and immediately thereafter shall cause to be prepared a certificate of the election containing an acceptance of the office, signed, sealed, and acknowledged by the new Trustee, which shall be in a form acceptable for recording in the registries of deeds of all the counties in which properties held under this instrument are situated.

    c. Whenever a new Trustee shall have been elected or appointed to the office of Trustee and shall have assumed the duties of office, he shall succeed to the title of all the properties of the Trust and shall have all the powers and be subject to all the restrictions granted to or imposed upon the Trustee by this agreement, and every Trustee shall have the powers, rights, and interests regarding the Trust Property, and shall be subject to the same restrictions and duties as the original Trustee, except as the same shall have been modified by amendment, as herein provided for.

    d. Notwithstanding any such resignation, the Trustee shall continue to have a lien on the Trust Property for all costs, expenses and attorney fees incurred and for said Trustee's reasonable compensation.

11. **Objects and Purposes of Trust.** The objects and purposes of this Trust shall be to hold title to the Trust Property and to protect and conserve it until its sale or other disposition or liquidation. The Trustee shall not undertake any activity not strictly necessary to the attainment of the foregoing objects and purposes, nor

shall The Trustee transact business within the meaning of applicable state law, or any other law, nor shall this Agreement be deemed to be, or create or evidence the existence of a corporation, de facto or de jure, or a Massachusetts Trust, or any other type of business trust, or an association in the nature of a corporation, or a partnership or joint venture by or between the Trustee and the Beneficiary, or by or between the Beneficiary.

12. **Exculpation.** The Trustee shall have no power to bind the Beneficiary personally and, in every written contract he may enter into, reference shall be made to this declaration; and any person or corporation contracting with, the Trustee, as well as any beneficiary, shall look to the funds and the Trust Property for payment under such contract,, or for the payment of any debt, mortgage, judgment, or decree, or for any money that may otherwise become due or payable, whether by reason or failure of the Trustee to perform the contract, or for any other reason, and neither the Trustee nor the Beneficiary shall be liable personally therefor.

13. **Dealings with Trustee.** No party dealing with the Trustee in relation to the Trust Property in any manner whatsoever, and, without limiting the foregoing, no party to whom the property or any part of it or any interest in it shall be conveyed, contracted to be sold, leased, or mortgaged by the Trustee, shall be obliged to see to the application of any purchase money, rent, or money borrowed or otherwise advanced on the property; to see that the terms of this Trust Agreement have been complied with; to inquire into the authority, necessity, or expediency of any act of the Trustee, or be privileged to inquire into any of the terms of this Trust Agreement. Every deed, mortgage, lease, or other instrument executed by the Trustee in relation to the Trust Property shall be conclusive evidence in favor of every person claiming any right, title, or interest under the Trust that at the time of its delivery the Trust created under this Agreement was in full force and effect; and that instrument was executed in accordance with the terms and conditions of this agreement and all its amendments, if any, and is binding upon all Beneficiary under it; that the Trustee was duly authorized and empowered to execute and deliver every such instrument; if a conveyance has been made to a successor or successors in trust, that the successor or successors have been appointed properly and are vested fully with all the title, estate, rights, powers, duties, and obligations of its, his, or their predecessor in Trust.

14. **Recording of Agreement.** This Agreement shall not be placed on record in the county in which the Trust Property is situated, or elsewhere, but if it is so recorded, that recording shall not be considered as notice of the rights of any person under this Agreement derogatory to the title of powers of the Trustee.

15. **Name of Trustee.** The name of the Trust shall not be used by the Beneficiary in connection with any advertising or other publicity whatsoever without the written consent of the Trustee.

16. **Income Tax Returns.** The Trustee shall be obligated to file any income tax returns with respect to the Trust, as required by law, and the Beneficiary individ-

ually shall report and pay their share of income taxes on the earnings and avails of the Trust Property or growing out of their interest under this Trust.

17. **Assignment.** The interest of a Beneficiary, of any part of that interest, may be transferred only by a written assignment executed in duplicate and delivered to the Trustee. The Trustee shall note his acceptance on the original and duplicate original of the assignment retaining the original and delivering the duplicate original to the assignee as and for his of her evidence of ownership of a beneficial interest under this Agreement. No assignment of any interest under this Agreement,, other than by operation of law that is not so executed, delivered, and accepted shall be valid without the written approval of all of the other Beneficiaries, if any, who possess the power of direction. No person who is vested with the power of direction, but who is not a Beneficiary under this Agreement, shall assign that power without the written consent of all the Beneficiary.

18. **Individual Liability of Trustee.** The Trustee shall not be required, in dealing with the Trust Property or in otherwise acting under this Agreement, to enter into any individual contract or other individual obligation whatsoever; nor to make himself individually liable to pay or incur the payment of any damages, attorney fees, fines, penalties, forfeitures, costs, charges, or other sums of money whatsoever. The Trustee shall have no individual liability or obligation whatsoever arising from its ownership, as Trustee, of the legal title to the Trust Property, or with respect to any act done or contract entered into or indebtedness incurred by him in dealing with the Trust Property or in otherwise acting under this Agreement, except only as f ar as the Trust Property and any trust funds in the actual possession of the Trustee shall be applicable to the payment and discharge of that liability or obligation.

19. **Reimbursement and Indemnification of Trustee.** If the Trustee shall pay or incur any liability to pay any money on account of this Trust, or incur any liability to pay any money on account of being made a party to any litigation as a result of holding title to the Trust Property or otherwise in connection with this Trust, whether because of breach of contract, injury to person or property, fines or penalties under any law, or otherwise, the Beneficiaries, jointly and severally agree that on demand they will pay to the Trustee, with interest at the maximum rate allowed under the laws of the State of Tennessee per annum, all such payments made or liabilities incurred by the Trustee, together with its expenses, including reasonable attorneys, fees, and that they will indemnify and hold the Trustee harmless of and from any and all payments made or liabilities incurred by him for any reason whatsoever as a result of this Agreement; and all amounts so paid by the Trustee, as well as his compensation under this Agreement, shall constitute a lien on the Trust Property. The Trustee shall not be required to convey or otherwise deal with Trust Property as long as any money is due to the Trustee under this Agreement; nor shall the Trustee be required to advance or pay out any money on account of this Trust or to prosecute or defend any legal proceedings involving this Trust or any property or interest under this Agreement unless he shall be furnished with sufficient funds or be indemnified to his satisfaction.

20. **Entire Agreement.** This Agreement contains the entire understanding between the parties and may be amended, revoked, or terminated only by written agreement signed by the Trustee and all of the Beneficiaries.

21. **Governing Law.** This Agreement, and all transactions contemplated hereby, shall be governed by, construed and enforced in accordance with the laws of the State of Tennessee applicable to contracts executed and performed in Tennessee. The parties waive any right to a trial by jury and agree to submit to the personal jurisdiction and venue of a court of subject matter jurisdiction location in _____ County, State of _____. In the event that litigation results from or arise out of the agreement or the performance thereof, the parties agree to reimburse the prevailing party's reasonable attorney fees, court costs, and all other expenses, whether or not taxable by the court as costs, in addition to any other relief to which the prevailing party may be entitled. In such event, no action shall be entertained by said court or any court of competent jurisdiction if filed more than one year subsequent to the date the cause(s) of action actually accrued regardless of whether damages were otherwise, as of said time, calculable.

22. **Binding Effect.** The terms and conditions of this agreement shall inure to the benefit of and be binding upon any successor Trustee under it, as well as upon the executors, administrators, heirs, assigns, and all other successors-in-interest of the beneficiary.

23. **Trustee's Liability to Beneficiaries.** The trustee shall be liable to the beneficiaries for the value of their respective beneficial interests only to the extent of the property held in trust by him hereunder and the beneficiaries shall enforce such liability only against the trust property and not against the trustee personally.

24. **Annual Statements.** There shall be no annual meeting of the beneficiaries, but the trustee shall prepare an annual report of their receipts and disbursements for the preceding fiscal year, which fiscal year shall coincide with the calendar year, and a copy of the report shall be sent by mail to the beneficiaries not later than February 28 of each year.

25. **Termination.** This Trust may terminate at any time by a majority of the beneficiaries and within thirty (30) days' written notice of termination delivered to the Trustee, and the Trustee shall execute any and all documents necessary to vest fee simple marketable title to any and all Trust Property in the Beneficiary.

In Witness Whereof, the parties hereto have executed this agreement as of the day and year first above written.

Beneficiary:

_____

Robert D. Shemin

_____

STATE OF TENNESSEE
COUNTY OF DAVIDSON

Personally appeared before me, _____, a Notary Public in and for the State and County aforesaid, Robert D. Shemin, the within named bargainer, with whom I am personally acquainted (or proved to me on the basis of satisfactory evidence), and who acknowledged that he executed the foregoing instrument for the purposes therein contained.

WITNESS my hand and seal at office, on this _____ day of October, 200___.

_____
Notary Public

My Commission Expires:

_____

STATE OF TENNESSEE
COUNTY OF _____

Personally appeared before me, _____, a Notary Public in and for the State and County aforesaid, _____, the within named bargainer, with whom I am personally acquainted (or proved to me on the basis of satisfactory evidence), and who acknowledged that he executed the foregoing instrument for the purposes therein contained.

WITNESS my hand and seal at office, on this _____ day of October, 200___.

Notary Public:_____

My Commission Expires:

_____

EXHIBIT A

LEGAL DESCRIPTION

EXHIBIT B

BENEFICIARIES AND THEIR INTERESTS

Name and Address   Interest

Robert D. Shemin

_____

_____   100%

LAND INSTALLMENT CONTRACT

THIS AGREEMENT made and entered into by and between

hereinafter called the Vendor and

hereinafter called the Vendee.

WITNESSETH: The Vendor, for himself, his heirs, and assigns, does hereby agree to sell to the Vendee, his heirs, and assigns, the following described real estate

together with all appurtenances, rights, privileges, and easements, and all buildings and fixtures in their present condition located upon said property.

1. CONTRACT PRICE, METHOD OF PAYMENT, INTEREST RATE
   In consideration whereof, the Vendee agrees to purchase the above described property for the sum of _____ Dollars ($_____), payable as follows:

   The sum of $_____ as down payment at the time of execution of the within Land Installment Contract the receipt of which is hereby acknowledged, leaving a principal balance owed by Vendee of $_____ together with interest on the unpaid balance payable in consecutive monthly installments of $_____ beginning on the _____ day of _____ 200__, and on the _____ day of each and every month thereafter until said balance and interest is paid in full, or until the _____ day of _____, whichever event occurs first. The interest on the unpaid balance due hereon shall be _____ (%) percent annum computed monthly, in accordance with a(n) _____ month amortization schedule during the life of this Contract.

   Payments shall be credited first to the interest, and the remainder to the to the principal or other sums due Vendor. The total amount of this obligation, both principal and interest, unpaid after making any such application of payments as herein receipted shall be the interest bearing principal amount of this obligation for the next succeeding interest computation period. If any payment is not received within _____ days of payment date, there shall be a late charge of _____ (__%) percent assessed. The Vendee may pay the entire purchase price on this contract without prepayment penalty. The monthly installments shall be payable as directed by the Vendor herein.

2. ENCUMBRANCES:
   Said real estate is presently subject to a mortgage and the Vendor shall not place any additional mortgage on the premises without the first written permission of the Vendee. In the event the Vendor should become delinquent in payments on the

mortgage, the Vendee may pay the same and credit said payment to the Contract price.

3. EVIDENCE OF TITLE:
The Vendor shall be required to provide an abstract or guarantee of title, statement of title, title insurance, or such other evidence of title.

4. RECORDING OF CONTRACT:
The Vendor shall cause a copy of this Contract to be recorded in the _____ County Recorder's Office within a period of twenty (20) days after the execution of this Contract by the parties hereto.

5. REAL ESTATE TAXES:
Real estate taxes shall be prorated to the date of the closing using the short-term method of tax proration being those becoming due and payable on _____, 200___. When the real estate taxes become due and payable, the Vendee shall pay same directly to the _____ County Treasurer and provide proof of payment to the Vendor.

6. INSURANCE AND MAINTENANCE:
The Vendee shall keep the premises insured for at least _____ thousand Dollars ($_____) against fire and extended coverage for the benefit of both parties, as their interest may appear, and provide a copy of the said policy to the Vendor or any mortgagee.

The Vendee shall keep the building in a good state of repair at the Vendee's expense. At such time as the Vendor inspects the premises and finds that repairs are necessary, Vendor shall request that these repairs be made within sixty (60) days at the Vendee's expense.

The Vendee has inspected the premises constituting the subject matter of this Land Installment Contract, and no representations have been made to the Vendee by the Vendor in regard to the condition of said premises; and it is agreed that the said premises are being sold to the Vendee as the same now exists and that the Vendor shall have no obligation to do or furnish anything toward the improvement of said premises. Vendor shall furnish a clear termite report at Vendor's expense prior to executing this Contract. If the property has live infestation of wood-destroying organisms, Vendor will pay costs of treatment and repair damages caused by same. If Vendor elects not to do so, Vendee may elect to waive Vendors responsibility and proceed, or Vendee may elect not to proceed with this Contract.

7. POSSESSION:
The Vendee shall be given possession of the above described premises at Contract execution and shall thereafter have and hold the same subject to the provisions for default hereinafter set forth.

8. DELIVERY OF DEED:

Upon full payment of this Contract, Vendor shall issue a General Warranty deed to the Vendee, free of all encumbrances except as otherwise set forth. In addition, Vendee reserves the right to convert this Contract into a note and mortgage and receive a Warranty Deed to Vendee or assigns from Vendor, anytime the following conditions have been met by the Vendee:

(1) At least 20% of the purchase price has been paid to Vendor.

(2) Vendee is willing to pay all the costs of title transfer and document preparations.

The note and mortgage will bear the same terms as this Contract for the remaining balance.

9. DEFAULT BY VENDEE:

If an installment payment to be made by the Vendee under the terms of this Land Contract is not paid by the Vendee when due or within two (2) installments thereafter, the entire unpaid balance shall become due and collectable at the election of the Vendor and the Vendor shall be entitled to all the remedies provided for by the laws of this state and/or to do any other remedies and/or relief now or hereafter provided for by law to such Vendor; and in the event of the breach of this Contract and any other respect by the Vendee, Vendor shall be entitled to all relief now or hereinafter provided for by the laws of this state.

Waiver by the Vendor of a default or a number of defaults in the performance hereof by the Vendee shall not be construed as a waiver of any default, no matter how similar.

10. GENERAL PROVISIONS:

There are no known pending orders issued by any governmental authority with respect to this property other than those spelled out in the Land Installment Contract prior to closing date for execution of the contract.

It is agreed that this Land Installment Contract shall be binding upon each of the parties, their administrators, executors, legal representatives, heirs, and assigns.

IN WITNESS WHEREOF, the parties have set their hands this _____ day of _____ 200___.

Signed in the presence of: VENDOR(S):

_____   _____

_____   _____

Signed in the presence of: VENDEE(S):

_____   _____

_____   _____

STATE OF _____

COUNTY OF _____

On this _____ day of _____ 200___, before me, a Notary Public in and for said county and state, personally came, _____ Vendor(s) and _____ Vendee(s) in the foregoing Land Installment Contract, and acknowledged and signing thereof to be their voluntary act and deed.

WITNESS my official signature and seal on the day last above mentioned.

NOTARY PUBLIC _____

PROMISSORY NOTE

$ _____   Dated: _____

Principal Amount: _____   State of: _____

FOR VALUE RECEIVED, the undersigned hereby jointly and severally promise to pay to the order of _____, the sum of _____ Dollars ($_____), together with interest thereon at the rate of _____ (%) per-cent per annum on the unpaid balance. Said sum shall be paid in the manner following:

All payments shall be first applied to interest and the balance to principal. This note may be prepaid, at any time, in whole or in part, without penalty. All prepayments shall be applied in reverse order of maturity.

This note shall at the option of any holder hereof be immediately due and payable upon the failure to make any payment due hereunder within _____ days of its due date.

In the event this note shall be in default, and placed with an attorney for collection, then the undersigned agree to pay all reasonable attorney fees and costs of collection. Payments not made within five (5) days of due date shall be subject to a late charge of _____ (%) percent of said payment. All payments hereunder shall be made to such address as may from time to time be designated by any holder hereof.

The undersigned and all other parties to this note, whether as endorsers, guarantors or sureties, agree to remain fully bound hereunder until this note shall be fully paid and waive demand, presentment and protest and all notices thereto and further agree to remain bound, notwithstanding any extension, renewal, modification, waiver, or other indulgence by any holder or upon the discharge or release of any obligor hereunder or to this note or upon the exchange, substitution, or release of any collateral granted as security for this note. No modification or indulgence by any hereof shall be binding unless in writing; and any indulgence on any one occasion shall not be an indulgence for any other or future occasion. Any modification or change of terms hereunder granted by any holder hereof, shall be valid and binding upon each of the undersigned, notwithstanding the acknowledgement of any of the undersigned, and each of the undersigned does hereby irrevocably grant to each of the others a power of attorney to enter into any such modification on their behalf. The rights of any holder hereof shall be cumulative and not necessarily successive. This note shall take effect as a sealed instrument and shall be construed, governed, and enforced in accordance with the laws of the State first appearing at the head of this note. The undersigned hereby execute this note as principals and not as sureties.

Signed in the presence of:

_____   _____

_____   _____

GUARANTY

We the undersigned jointly and severally guaranty the prompt and punctual payment of all monies due under the aforesaid now and agree to remain bound until fully paid.

In the presence of:

_____   _____

_____   _____

QUITCLAIM DEED

ADDRESS new owners: as follows	SEND TAX BILLS to:	MAP PARCEL number:
_____ Name	_____ Name	_____
_____ Street Address or Route Number	_____ Street Address or Route Number	_____
_____ City State Zip	_____ City State Zip	_____

FOR AND IN CONSIDERATION of One Dollar ($1.00), cash in hand paid, the receipt of which is hereby acknowledged, _____, by these presents do hereby quitclaim and convey unto _____ successors and assigns, all _____ rights, title, and interest in and to the following described tract of land;

STATE OF _____
COUNTY OF _____

The actual consideration for this transfer is $_____. Subscribed and sworn to before me this the _____ day of _____, 200____.

My commission expires _____
                                      (Affix Seal)   Notary Public

Said property is conveyed subject to such limitations, restrictions, and encumbrances as may affect the premises.

Witness _____ hand _____ this _____ day of _____, 200___, the corporate party, if any, having caused its name to be signed hereto by its duly authorized officers on said day and date.

_____   _____

WARRANTY DEED TO TRUSTEE

The Grantor(s) _____ of the County of _____ and the State of _____ for and in consideration $ _____ Dollars, and other good and valuable considerations in hand paid, conveys, grants, bargains, sells, aliens, remises, releases, confirms, and warrants under provisions of Section _____.

Unto _____ as Trustee and not personally under the provisions of a Trust Agreement dated the _____ day of _____ 200___, known as Trust Number _____, the following described real estate in the County of State of, to wit:

Together with all the tenements, hereditaments, and appurtenances thereto, belonging or in anywise appertaining.

To have and to hold the said premises in fee simple forever, with the appurtenances attached thereto upon the trust and for the uses and purposes herein and in said Trust Agreement set forth.

Full power and authority granted to said Trustee, with respect to the said premises or any part of it, and at any time or times, to subdivide said premises or any part thereof, to dedicate parks, streets, highways, or alleys and to vacate any subdivision or part thereof, and to resubdivide said property as often as desired, to contract to sell, to grant options to purchase, to sell on any terms to convey either with or without consideration, to donate, to mortgage, to pledge, or otherwise encumber said property, or any part thereof to lease said property, or any part, from time to time, in possession or reversion by leases to commence now or later and upon any terms and for any period or periods of time and to renew or extend leases upon any terms and for any period or periods of time to renew of extend leases upon any terms and for any period or periods of time, and to amend, change, or modify the terms and provisions thereof at any time hereafter, to contract to make leases and to grant options to lease and options to renew leases and options to purchase the whole or any part of the reversion and to contract respecting the manner of fixing the amount of future renters to partition or to exchange the said property or any part thereof for other real or personal property, to grant easements or changes of any kind, to release, convey, or assign any right, title, or interest in or about easement appurtenant to said premises or any part, and to deal with said property and every part thereof in all other ways and for such other considerations as it would be lawful for any person owning the same to deal with the same, whether similar to or different from the ways above specified, at any time or times hereafter.

In no case shall any party dealing with the said Trustee in relation to said premises, to whom said premises or any part thereof shall be conveyed, contracted to be sold, leased, or mortgaged by said trustee, be obliged to see to the application of any purchase money, rent, or money borrowed or advanced on said premises, or be obliged to see that the terms of this Trust have been complied with, or be obliged to inquire into the necessity or expediency of any act of said Trustee, or be obliged or privileged to inquire into any terms of said Trust Agreement; and every deed, mortgage, lease, or other instrument executed by said Trustee in relation to said real estate shall be conclusive evidence in favor of every person relying upon or claiming under such conveyance, lease, or other instrument, (a) that at the same time of delivery thereof, the Trust created by this Indenture and by said Trust Agreement was in full force and effect, (b) that such conveyance or other instrument was executed in full accordance if the Trust's constitutions and limitations contained herein and thereunder Trust Agreement or in some amendment thereof and binding upon all beneficiaries thereunder and (c) that said Trustee was duly authorized and empowered to execute and deliver every such deed, trust deed, lease, mortgage, and other instrument.

The interest of each and every beneficiary hereunder and of all persons claiming under them or any of them shall be only in the earning, avails, and proceeds arising from the sale or other disposition of said real estate, and such interest is hereby declared to be personal property. No beneficiary hereunder shall have any title or interest legal or equitable, in or to said real estate as such, but only an interest in the earnings, avails, and proceeds thereof as aforesaid.

And the Grantor hereby covenants with said Grantee that the Grantor is lawfully seized of said land in fee simple, that the Grantor has good right and lawful authority to sell and convey said land and will defend the same against the lawful claims of any persons whomsoever, and that the said land is free of all encumbrances, except taxes accruing subsequent to December 31.

In witness whereof, the said Grantor has hereunto set their hands and seals this _____ day of _____, 200___.

Signed, Sealed, and Delivered in our presence:

_____   _____

Seal

_____   _____

Seal

State of _____   County of _____

I hereby certify that on this day, before me, an officer duly authorized in the State aforesaid to take acknowledgments, personally appeared _____ to me known as the person(s) described in and who executed the foregoing Instrument and _____ _____ acknowledged before me that executed the same.

Witness my hand and official seal in the County and State aforesaid this _____ day of _____ , 200___ .

Notary Public _____

My commission expires: _____

DISCLOSURE FORM

I, _____ , acknowledge that _____ is a licensed real estate agent with COMPANY NAME and is buying/selling this property for investment purposes. I further acknowledge that _____ may rent out or resell this property at a later date for a profit.

I agree to hold _____ and COMPANY NAME harmless for any claims that I may have regarding this contract. Also, I acknowledge that neither _____ or COMPANY NAME represent me or my interests.

DATE _____

BUYER _____

SELLER _____

SAMPLE NOTICE OF FORECLOSURE
(Example Only)

Default having occurred in the terms, condition, and payments as provided for in a certain Deed of Trust executed by _____ (name), dated _____, recorded in Book _____, page _____, Register's Office for _____ (County), _____ (State), to secure the indebtedness therein described, and said indebtedness being due and unpaid, the whole thereof having been declared due and payable as provided in said Deed of Trust, notice is hereby given that I, _____ _____ (Your name), Trustee, under the power and authority vested in me by said instrument and having been so requested by the lawful holder and owner of said indebtedness, will on THE _____ DAY OF_____ , 200___ , at _____ (time of day) at the (north, south, east, west) door of the Courthouse in _____ (County), _____ (State), sell at public outcry to the highest bidder for cash, and free from the equity of redemption, homestead, dower, and all other exemptions of every land, all of which are expressly waived in said Deed of Trust, the following land:

Said sale will be subject to any and all unpaid taxes and all other liens that take priority over this Deed of Trust up on which the Foreclosure sale is had. This property is known as _____ (address of property).

_____
                  (Your Name, Address, and Telephone)
Insertion Dates: _____ , _____ , and _____

Forms for Landlords

Use these forms to help prepare apartments and screen prospective tenants. Feel free to use or copy any of them. However, consult your attorney and/or accountant before relying on these documents or any of the information contained in them.

Rental Unit Preparation
Management Move-In Checklist
Vacancy Makeover Checklist
Rental Application
Lease-Option Prospect Qualify Form
Lease Agreement
Security Deposit Policy
Maintenance Guarantee
Maintenance Request

RENTAL UNIT PREPARATION (for office use)

Inspector's Initials:

NEW LOCKS

PAINTING

WINDOWS PATCHED

CARPETS CLEANED

APPLIANCES OPERATING/CLEANED

ELECTRICAL OUTLETS/FIXTURES

WATER PIPES/TOILETS CHECKED FOR LEAKS

YARDS CUT AND DEBRIS PICKED UP

PEST CONTROL SPRAYED

STAIRS, HANDRAILS, PORCHES REPAIRED

SMOKE ALARM TESTED

NICE CLEAN SMELL PRESENT

DRAPES OR BLINDS HUNG AT WINDOWS

ANY SPECIAL ADDED TOUCHES

WELCOME CARD LEFT FOR NEW TENANT

Date of Inspection:

MANAGEMENT MOVE-IN CHECKLIST

ADDRESS:

TENANT'S NAME:

DATE:

Application filled out and fee collected:

Verification filled out and fee collected:

Deposit given to reserve rental:

First month's rent collected:

Security deposit collected:

Move-in payment schedule:

Rental Agreement signed and explained:

Additional agreements:

Information sheet for new tenants:

On-time payments emphasized/collection procedures:

Rental inventory sheet given and checked:

Office hours/maintenance:

Request/repair policies explained:

Periodic inspections discussed:

Renter's insurance suggested:

VACANCY MAKEOVER CHECKLIST

1. Check and test all wall receptacles and switches. One faulty switch affects the overall safety of the electrical system.

2. Turn on/off all faucets. Check for leaks, also around the tub, showerheads, and under sink.

3. Flush toilets. Make sure they are functioning properly, no leaks around bottom, maintain water, and shut off properly.

4. Close and open all doors—exterior, interior, sliding, and closets. Check door stops.

5. If drapes are provided, clean or order replacements.

6. Clean and vacuum all carpets.

7. Exterminate for all pests.

8. Replace light bulbs if out. Good lighting helps show vacant units.

9. Clean and check in, behind, and under all appliances. Make sure all appliances are running effectively.

10. Make sure all countertops, drawers, and cabinets are clean. Remove old shelf paper. Check to see that all hardware is in place.

11. Make bathrooms shine (tubs, sink, mirrors, all tile, medicine cabinets, and vanities). Remove any decals, etc. Paint if necessary.

12. Make sure all bathroom details are in place (towel bars, toilet paper holders, soap dishes).

13. Check condition of paint on all interior walls/ceilings. Paint if necessary. Fill in any holes.

14. Clean and shine all vinyl flooring.

15. Clean all windows and mirrors. Replace any broken or scratched windows. Check to see if all screens are in place and whether they are torn.

16. Check heating units and air conditioners, including replacing filters.

17. Remove all debris or personal items left.

18. Put air freshener in place.

19. Sweep entryways and wash off front of building/house. Does front porch need painting?

20. Re-key all locks and ensure all are working properly. See if any window locks are needed.

21. Is exterior of premises clean and neat? Does grass need cutting or other landscaping needs?

Checklist Complete: Date:

RENTAL APPLICATION

Applicant Wants to Lease _____

Applicant Wants to Move In _____

Application Fee _____

Date of Application _____ Applicant's Name _____

Social Security #_____ Children's Names & Ages _____

Present Address _____ How Long? _____

Present Landlord's Name _____ Phone # _____

Previous Address _____ How Long? _____

Previous Landlord's Name _____ Phone # _____

Have you ever paid the rent late? _____ Why? _____

Employer _____ Employer Address _____

Supervisor _____ Your Job Title _____

Length of Service _____ Salary per Week _____

Supervisor's Phone # _____ Any arrest record? _____

Credit References with Phones:

1. _____

2. _____

3. _____

Car Financed? _____ Name of Company _____ Address _____

Furniture Financed? _____ Name of Company _____ Address _____

Applicant's Driver's License # _____ State _____

MDHA Case Worker _____

In Case of an Emergency

Name _____ Address _____ Phone # _____

Relation _____ Doctor's Name _____

I hereby authorize _____ to submit the information I have given for verification and I specifically authorize _____ to contact the employers, landlords, banks, police for any police records, and other credit references that I have listed above for the purpose of verifying the information furnished by me in this application.

_____
Applicant's Signature

LEASE-OPTION PROSPECT QUALIFY FORM

NAME: _____ Date/Time _____

Phone _____ Regarding _____ Rating _____

2nd Applicant Name: _____ Other Applicants _____ Pets _____

Are you looking to rent or own? _____ Have you seen the house? _____

Where do you live now (house or apt.)? _____ How long there? _____

How much do you pay now? _____ Have you ever been evicted/late pay? _____

Is your landlord aware that you will be moving? _____

Employer/Position _____ How long there? _____ Gross there is: _____

Spouse Emp./Pos. _____ How long there? _____ Gross there is: _____

How is your credit? _____ How is your spouse's credit? _____

When can you move in? _____ What is the most you can pay per month? _____

How much money do you have to put down on your new home? _____

Tax return _____ Can you pay extra/month to build up a down payment? _____

We know the bank requires this and you won't ever be able to buy if we don't work out a down payment plan.

We want you to succeed!

LEASE AGREEMENT

1. **PARTIES:** The parties to this agreement are **Superior Properties Corporation,** hereinafter referred to as "Landlord," and _____, and _____, hereinafter referred to as "Tenant(s)." All adult occupants of the subject premises must sign this Lease Agreement and each will be jointly and severally liable under the terms and conditions of said Agreement. Additional occupants of the premises will be _____ (Age_____); _____ (Age_____); and _____ (Age_____) only.

2. **PROPERTY:** Landlord hereby lets the following property to Tenant for the term of this agreement; the property located at and known as: _____, _____, _____, Tennessee.
        (City)   (County)

3. **TERM:** The term of the Agreement shall be for _____beginning on _____ and ending on _____.

4. **RENT:** The monthly/weekly rental for said property shall be $ _____ per month/week. One full month's/week's rent shall be paid upon execution of this Agreement. Rent for the second month/week is the prorated amount of $_____, and is due and payable on the _____ day of _____, 200_____. The remaining payments are to be paid consecutively on the first day of each month/week (Saturday) at such place as the Landlord shall direct. NOTICE OF TERMINATION OF TENANCY UNDER LEASE AGREEMENT FOR NON-PAYMENT OF RENT IS HEREBY SPECIFICALLY WAIVED.

5. **LATE CHARGES:** Any rent installment that is paid more than five (5) days after its due date shall include a late charge of 10% (ten percent) of the rent installment. Said late charges shall become a separate portion of rent due under the Terms and Conditions of this Lease.

6. **RETURN CHECK CHARGES:** A charge of $25 shall be paid by Tenant for any check that is returned unpaid. Upon return or dishonor of any check tendered as payment of rent, late charges will be assessed as if no rental payment was attempted.

7. **UTILITIES, APPLIANCES & OTHER ITEMS FURNISHED BY LANDLORD:**

   Utilities shall be paid by the party indicated on the following chart:

	LANDLORD	TENANT
Electricity	_____	_____
Gas	_____	_____
Water	_____	_____
Garbage	_____	_____
Other	_____	_____

Appliances furnished to Tenant by Landlord:

	YES	NO
Refrigerator	_____	_____
Stove	_____	_____
Air Conditioner	_____	_____
Dishwasher	_____	_____

Yard care shall be the responsibility of the Landlord/Tenant.

When electricity, gas, or water is to be furnished by Landlord, Tenant agrees not to use any supplemental heating or air-conditioning units, clothes or dishwashing machines, or clothes dryers, other than those furnished by Landlord and above listed. Due to the high utility costs involving use of such units or appliances, Tenant agrees to obtain prior written approval before using or connecting such supplemental units or appliances.

Tenant agrees that any unauthorized use of supplemental heating or air-conditioning units, clothes or dishwashing machines, or clothes dryers, other than those furnished by Landlord and above listed shall increase the monthly/weekly rental for the subject property at the rate of per month or per week. Said increase shall be automatic upon discovery of any of the above mentioned units or appliances, without any notice required, and shall continue for the full term of this Lease. Said increase shall become a portion of rent due under the Terms and Conditions of this Agreement

8. **USE OF PROPERTY, OCCUPANTS, AND GUESTS:** Tenant shall use the subject property for residential purposes only. The property shall be occupied only by those Tenants listed in item one (1). PARTIES, of this Lease.

9. **TENANT'S DUTY TO MAINTAIN PREMISES:** Tenant shall keep the dwelling unit in a clean and sanitary condition and shall otherwise comply with all state and local laws requiring tenants to maintain rented premises. If damage to the dwelling unit other than normal wear and tear is caused by acts or negligence of Tenant or others occupying the premises under his/her control, Landlord may cause such repairs to be made, and Tenant shall be liable to Landlord for any reasonable expenses thereby incurred by Landlord.

10. **ALTERATIONS:** No alteration, addition, or improvements shall be made by Tenant in or to the dwelling unit without the prior written consent of Landlord. Such consent shall be totally at Landlord's option.

11. **NOISE:** Tenant agrees not to allow on the premises any excessive noise or other activity that disturbs the peace and quiet of others.

12. **INSPECTION BY LANDLORD:** The Tenant agrees to allow Landlord to enter the subject premises in order to inspect the premises, make necessary or agreed repairs, decorations, alterations, or improvements, supply necessary or agreed services, or exhibit the dwelling unit to prospective or actual purchasers, mortgag-

ees, tenants, workmen, or contractors. The Landlord may enter the dwelling unit without consent to Tenant in case of emergency.

13. **SECURITY DEPOSIT:** Tenant agrees to deposit with Landlord upon execution of the Lease Contract, receipt of which is hereby acknowledged, the sum of $_____ Dollars. This deposit is held as security against any damage to the entire property, including but not limited to furniture, appliances, fixtures, and carpet; and Tenant vacating the entire premises prior to the termination date of this Lease, or failing to perform any and all the covenants herein. Said deposit is neither an advance rental payment nor a bonus to the Landlord, and Landlord agrees that if all the covenants imposed upon Tenant have been fulfilled, Landlord shall refund said deposit by mail to the address furnished by the Tenant, after the premises have been vacated by Tenant and inspected by Landlord as provided by statute. Said deposit shall be deposited in _____ Bank.

14. **LIEN:** The Tenant hereby gives Landlord a lien upon all his personal property situated upon said premises, including all furniture and household furnishings. This lien is for the rent agreed to be paid hereunder, for any damage caused by Tenant beyond normal wear and tear, and for Court costs and attorney fees incurred under the Terms and Conditions of this Agreement.

15. **SUBLEASING:** Tenant shall not assign this Agreement or sublet the dwelling unit without prior written consent of Landlord. Such consent shall be totally at Landlord's option.

16. **PERSONAL INJURY AND PROPERTY DAMAGE:** Subject to standards required by law, neither Landlord nor its principal shall be liable to Tenant, his family, employees, or guests, for any damage to person or property caused by the acts or omissions of other Tenants or other persons, whether such persons be off the property of Landlord or on the property with or without permission of Landlord; nor shall Landlord be liable for losses or damages from theft, fire, water, rain, storm, explosion, sonic boom, or other causes whatsoever, nor shall Landlord be liable for loss or damages resulting from failure, interruption, or malfunctions in the utilities provided to Tenant under this Lease Agreement; nor shall Landlord be liable for injuries elsewhere on the premises.

LANDLORD IS NOT RESPONSIBLE FOR, AND WILL NOT PROVIDE, FIRE OR CASUALTY INSURANCE FOR THE TENANT'S PERSONAL PROPERTY.

In further consideration of this Agreement, Tenant agrees that, subject to standards required by law, Landlord does not warrant the condition of the premises in any respect, and his liability for any injury to the Tenant, his family, agent, or those claiming under him, or those on the premises by his or their invitation, shall be limited to injuries arising from such defects that are unknown by claimant and are known to Landlord or are willfully concealed by him. Additionally, Tenant has inspected the premises and binds himself to hold Landlord harmless against any and all claims for damages arising from those who sustain injuries upon the above leased premises, during the term of this Lease, or any extension thereof.

17. **IN CASE OF MALFUNCTION OF EQUIPMENT, DAMAGE BY FIRE, WATER OR ACT OF GOD:** Tenant shall notify Landlord immediately of malfunction of equipment, damage by fire, water, or act of God and Landlord shall repair the damage with reasonable promptness, or if the premises are deemed by the Landlord to be damaged so much as to be unfit for occupancy, or if the Landlord decides not to repair or restore the building, this Lease shall terminate. If the Lease is so terminated, rent will be prorated on a daily basis so that Tenant will pay only to the date of the damage, and the remainder of the month will be refunded.

18. **PETS:** Tenant shall not permit a pet to live on the premises without signing and complying with the provisions of a separately negotiated Pet Agreement. All pets are subject to visual inspection and approval by Landlord at such times as Landlord may direct during normal working hours.

19. **TERMINATION—ALL TENANTS PLEASE TAKE NOTICE!** At least thirty (30) days prior to the termination date of this Lease Agreement, Tenant must give Landlord written notice of his intent to vacate the subject premises. Failure of Tenant to give Landlord said notice of intent to vacate the subject premises will cause Landlord to treat tenant as a holdover in accordance with item twenty (20.) **HOLDOVER,** of this Lease Agreement, no matter if Tenant continues to occupy the premises or not.

Upon proper termination or expiration of this Agreement, Tenant shall vacate the premises, remove all personal property belonging to him, and leave the premises as clean as he found them.

20. **HOLDOVER:** If Tenant holds over upon termination or expiration of this Agreement and/or Landlord accepts Tenant's tender of the monthly rent provided by this Agreement, this Agreement shall continue to be binding on the parties as a month-to-month agreement under the same Terms and Conditions as herein contained.

21. **ATTORNEY FEES:** Violation of any of the conditions of this Agreement shall be sufficient cause for eviction from said premises. Tenants agree to pay all costs of such action or cost of collection of damages as a result of Tenant's breach of this Agreement, including reasonable attorney fees.

22. **NOTICES:** All notices provided for by this Agreement shall be in writing and shall be given to the other party as follows: to Tenant, at the premises; to Landlord, at _____.

23. **MAINTENANCE REQUESTS:** Except in emergencies, all requests for maintenance must be made in writing to Landlord, at the following address: _____ _____.

24. **ABSENCE OR ABANDONMENT:** The Tenant must notify the Landlord of any extended absence from the premises in excess of seven (7) days. Notice shall be given on or before the first day of any extended absence. The Tenant's unexplained and/or extended absence from the premises for (30) days or more without payment of rent as due shall be prima facie evidence of abandonment. The Landlord is then expressly authorized to enter, remove, and store all personal items belonging to Tenant. If Tenant does not claim said personal property within an additional thirty (30) days, Landlord may sell or dispose of said personal property and apply the proceeds of said sale to the unpaid rent, damages, storage fees, sale costs, and attorney fees. Any unclaimed balance held by the Landlord for a period of six (6) months shall be forfeited to the Landlord.

25. **TERMINATION FOR VIOLENT OR DANGEROUS BEHAVIOR:** Landlord shall terminate this Lease Agreement within three (3) days from the date written notice is delivered to the Tenant if the Tenant or any other persons on the premises with the Tenant's consent willfully or intentionally commits a violent act or behaves in a manner that constitutes or threatens to be a real and present danger to the health, safety, or welfare of the life or property of others.

26. **BREACH OF LEASE:** If there is any other material noncompliance of the Lease Agreement by the Tenant, not previously specifically mentioned, or a noncompliance materially affecting health and safety, the Landlord may deliver a written notice to the Tenant specifying the acts and omissions constituting the breach, and that the Lease Agreement will terminate upon a date not less than thirty (30) days after receipt of the notice. If the breach is not remedied in fourteen (14) days, the Lease Agreement shall terminate as provided in the notice subject to the following: If the breach is remediable by repairs or the payment of damages or otherwise and the Tenant adequately remedies the breach prior to the date specified in the notice, the rental agreement will not terminate.

If the same act or omission that constituted a prior noncompliance, of which notice was given, recurs within six (6) months, the Landlord may terminate the Lease Agreement upon at least (14) days' written notice specifying the breach and the date of termination of the Lease Agreement.

27. **RULES AND REGULATIONS:** Tenant has read and agrees to abide by all Rules and Regulations of the Landlord as they presently exist or as they may be amended at Landlord's sole discretion. Said Rules and Regulations are attached hereto and are herein incorporated by reference.

28. **ALTERATIONS OR CHANGE IN THIS AGREEMENT:** It is expressly understood by Landlord and Tenant that the Terms and Conditions herein set out cannot be changed or modified, except in writing. Tenant understands that neither Tenant nor Landlord or any of Landlord's agents have the authority to modify this Lease Agreement except with a written instrument signed by all parties.

29. **APPLICATION:** Tenant's Application is an important part of this Lease, incorporated by reference and made a part hereof any misrepresentations, misleading or false statements made by Tenant and later discovered by the Landlord shall, at the option of the Landlord, void this Lease Agreement.

30. **SAVINGS CLAUSE:** If any provision of this Lease is determined to be in conflict with the law, thereby making said provision null and void, the nullity shall not affect the other provisions of this Lease, which can be given effect without the void provision, and to this end the provisions of the Lease are severable.

31. **TENANTS ARE RESPONSIBLE FOR THEIR OWN SECURITY:** Tenant hereby states that he has inspected the subject premises and has determined to his satisfaction that the smoke detectors, door locks and latches, window locks and latches, and any other security devices within the subject premises are adequate and in proper working order. Tenant acknowledges that Landlord is under no obligation or duty to inspect, test, or repair smoke detectors during Tenant's occupancy. Further, Tenant acknowledges that Landlord is under no obligation or duty to inspect, test, or repair any other security device unless and until Landlord has received written notice of disrepair of the device.

Tenant further acknowledges that neither Landlord nor his agents or representatives guarantee, warrant, or assume the personal security of Tenant. Tenant further acknowledges and understands that Tenant's personal safety and security is primarily Tenant's responsibility. In particular, Tenant recognizes that Tenant is in the best position to determine and foresee risks of loss and to protect himself and his property against such losses. In this regard, Tenant recognizes that any of Landlord's efforts are voluntary and not obligatory.

32. **ADDITIONAL TERMS AND CONDITIONS:** Additional paragraphs _____
through _____ are attached hereto and are part of this Lease Agreement.

Wherefore, we the undersigned do hereby execute and agree to this Lease Agreement, this _____ day of _____ , 200____.

President, Superior Properties Corp.   _____

LANDLORD   TENANT SS#_____

_____   _____

LANDLORD/MANAGER   TENANT SS#_____

RULES AND REGULATIONS
(Referred to in and made a part of the Parties' Lease Agreement)

1. No signs, notices, or advertisements shall be attached to or displayed by Tenant on or about said premises. Additionally, no antenna or satellite dish shall be attached to or displayed on or about the premises.

2. Profane, obscene, loud, or boisterous language, or unseemly behavior and conduct is absolutely prohibited, and Tenant obligates himself and those under him not to do or permit to be done anything that will annoy, harass, embarrass, or inconvenience any of the other tenants or occupants in the subject or adjoining premises.

3. No motor vehicle shall be kept upon the property that is unlicensed, inoperable, or in damaged condition. Damaged condition includes but is not limited to flat tires. Any such vehicle that remains on the property for more than ten (10) days after notice to remove same has been placed on subject vehicle shall be towed by wrecker and stored with a wrecker service at the Tenant's and/or the vehicle owner's expense.

4. In keeping with Fire Safety Standards, all motorized vehicles including motorcycles must be parked outside. No motorized vehicles shall be parked in any building structure on the property except authorized garage spaces.

5. In accordance with Fire Safety Standards and other safety regulations, no Tenant shall maintain or allow to be maintained, any auxiliary heating unit, air-conditioning units, or air filtering units without prior inspection and written approval of Landlord.

6. The sound of musical instruments, radios, televisions, phonographs, and singing shall at all times be limited in volume to a point that is not objectionable to other tenants or occupants in the subject or adjoining premises.

7. Only persons employed by Landlord or his agent shall adjust or have anything to do with the heating or air-conditioning plants or with the repair or adjustment of any plumbing, stove, refrigerator, dishwasher, or any other equipment that is furnished by Landlord or is part of the subject premises.

8. No awning, venetian blinds, or window guards shall be installed, except where prior approval is given by the Landlord.

9. Tenant shall not alter, replace, or add locks or bolts or install any other attachments, such as doorknockers, upon any door, except where prior approval is given by the Landlord

10. No defacement of the interior or exterior of the buildings or the surrounding grounds will be tolerated.

11. If furnished by Landlord, garbage disposal shall only be used in accordance with the disposal guidelines. All refuse shall be timely removed from the premises and placed outside in receptacles.

12. No spikes, hooks, or nails shall be driven into the walls, ceiling or woodwork of the leased premises without consent of Landlord. No crating of or boxing of furniture or other articles will be allowed within the leased premises.

13. It is specifically understood that Landlord reserves solely to itself the right to alter, amend, modify, and add rules to this Lease.

14. It is understood and agreed that Landlord shall not be responsible for items stored in storage areas.

15. Landlord has the right to immediately remove combustible material from the premises or any storage area.

16. Landlord will furnish one (1) key for each outside door of the premises. All keys must be returned to Landlord upon termination of the occupancy.

17. Lavatories, sinks, toilets, and all water and plumbing apparatus shall be used only for the purpose for which they were constructed. Sweepings, rubbish, rags, ashes, or other foreign substances shall not be thrown therein. Any damage to such apparatus and the cost of clearing plumbing resulting from misuse shall be the sole responsibility of and will be borne by Tenant.

_____   _____
TENANT   TENANT

_____   _____
TENANT   TENANT

SECURITY DEPOSIT POLICY

Refund of the security deposit referred to in the attached Lease Agreement is subject to compliance with all six (6) of the following provisions:

1. That a full term of the lease has expired;

2. That thirty (30) days' written notice is given, prior to vacating the subject premises at the end of said full term;

3. That there are no damages to Landlord's property, including but not limited to furniture, appliances, carpet, drapes, blinds, floor coverings;

4. That the entire apartment, including range, refrigerator, bathrooms, closets, and cupboards are clean;

5. That no late charges, delinquent rents, or fees for the damages remain unpaid;

6. That all keys, including mailbox keys, are returned to the Landlord.

The following questions and answers are for the purpose of eliminating misunderstandings concerning the security deposit:

1. Question: What charges will be deducted from the deposit if Tenant has failed to comply with all of the above listed six (6) conditions?

   Answer: The cost of all material and labor for cleaning the apartment and making repairs, all delinquent payments and fees, and all rental income lost as a result of Tenant vacating the premises prior to the termination date of his lease, or during any holdover period.

2. Question: What should Tenant be careful to avoid?

   Answer: (a) Damage to property, furniture, walls and wall coverings, appliances, carpet, drapes/blinds, and floor coverings. Departing Tenant will be held responsible for all damages beyond normal wear and tear. (b) Dirty appliances. Be sure to clean range and refrigerator.

3. Question: How is the Security Deposit returned?

   Answer: If Tenant has complied with all the terms and conditions concerning the Security Deposit, the deposit will be returned by check mailed to a forwarding address furnished to Landlord by Tenant.

NOTE: The Security Deposit may not be applied to the last monthly rental, or any other rent payment!

_____ _____
TENANT   TENANT

_____ _____
TENANT   TENANT

MAINTENANCE GUARANTEE

ATTENTION ALL NEW AND CURRENT RESIDENTS:

We now offer a maintenance guarantee to all residents. To ensure your satisfaction with our rental and the service we provide, we guarantee that all repairs that we are responsible for, as outlined in your lease, will be fixed within 72 hours so that the problem does not continue to create a hardship for you or your family.

If the problem or hardship is not corrected within the 72 hour period, you will have FREE RENT UNTIL THE PROBLEM IS CORRECTED on a per day basis following the third day, or 72-hour period. Your FREE RENT will be awarded in the form of a rent rebate following the next rental payment received.

RESIDENT: APPROVED BY:

ADDRESS: MOVE-IN DATE:

MAINTENANCE REQUEST

Date: Name:

Address: Telephone #:

Problem: How long in this condition?

Time and day we can inspect: Can we enter if you are not home?

DO NOT WRITE BELOW THIS LINE—FOR OFFICE USE ONLY

Date received: By:

Action taken: Date completed:

By: What was done:

Labor cost: Materials uscd:

Total cost:

Contractor Policies
and Procedures

Use this form to hire the best possible contractors and ensure the highest quality work. Feel free to use or copy it. However, consult your attorney and/or accountant before relying on these documents or any of the information contained in them.

CONTRACTOR POLICIES AND PROCEDURES

1. All proposed work to be performed for *COMPANY* will be submitted by written bid prior to any work being performed.

2. All part-time workers or bidders hired by *COMPANY* are independent subcontractors and are responsible for their own insurance and tax requirements. No worker or bidder shall hold *COMPANY* and Investment Corp. liable for any claims arising from any cause on any job. The liability for each job shall be the sole responsibility of the bidder alone.

3. NO check will be issued to any worker upon demand. Paid-on-completion jobs will be paid by check—AFTER inspection, after presentation of a proper invoice, within five (5) working days by mail.

4. NO checks will be mailed without an invoice.

5. NO checks will be written to walk-ins on demand.

6. Inspections are as follows: *NO EXCEPTIONS*
   ROOF: AFTER first significant rainfall or Metro Codes.
   ELECTRICAL: AFTER final inspection and white tag from Metro Codes.
   PLUMBING: AFTER full inspection of both supply and drain pipes and all fixtures or Metro Codes if applicable.
   HVAC: AFTER five days of continuous operation or verification of proper permit and subsequent final inspection by Metro Codes.
   HAULING/TRASH DISPOSAL: AFTER dump receipts and invoice(s) are furnished.
   METRO CODES INSPECTION MEANS: CLEARED AND RELEASED ON THEIR COMPUTER AND THE APPROPRIATE UTILITY.

7. All invoices should be mailed to *COMPANY* or left in the mailbox at COMPANY ADDRESS.

8. All calls from workers concerning the job or payment for work completed should be made during normal business hours, Monday through Friday, unless other instructions are given.

9. NO draws or advancements of any kind will be made to any worker for any reason other than those agreed on in a bid or other arrangement in writing.

NO EXCEPTIONS
DO NOT WALK IN AND REQUEST A CHECK—ALL CHECKS WILL BE MAILED

10. No tools will be furnished by *COMPANY* to any worker. Should an exception be made for an emergency, the worker is to be completely responsible for the tool(s). Should they be lost or damaged, *COMPANY* will deduct the amount necessary to replace the tool(s) from the workers' paycheck.

11. ALL BIDS must include a start date, estimate of time to complete, and a finish date. ALL BIDDERS must adjust their schedules to finish ON TIME. Work not performed within the bidders own agreed schedule will be penalized at a rate of (5%), five percent per day of the total bid until completion. *THIS WILL BE ENFORCED!*

12. Any bidder who pulls off in the middle of a job WILL BE LIABLE for any difference in his bid and what it costs *COMPANY* to finish the job, plus the (5%) five percent per day penalty until the job is restarted with a suitable replacement.

13. Any bidder who agrees to perform work for *COMPANY* will NOT be allowed to subcontract the work to someone else without the written permission of *COMPANY.* The bidder is to be on the job site to perform the work HIMSELF and oversee his helpers.

14. Should any bidder hire helpers, they shall be the sole responsibility of the bidder and he alone assumes all liability for them.

15. All work performed by bidder shall be in a quality workman-like manner. The use of substandard materials, fewer materials than considered normal, or any attempt to cover up poor workmanship or inferior materials will result in immediate termination of the bidder ON THE SPOT.

16. Any dispute over quality or workmanship will be resolved by the use of a for-hire independent inspectors' licensed contractor who is an expert in the category of the dispute, or a Metro Codes inspector.

17. The use, possession, presence, or the obvious effects of the use of any drugs or alcohol on any job site for *COMPANY* will be cause for IMMEDIATE TERMINATION—*NO EXCEPTIONS!*

18. Should any worker or bidder cause any damage to any part of the job site while performing their work, *COMPANY* will have the damage repaired and deduct that amount from the worker's paycheck.

THE FOLLOWING INFORMATION MUST BE COMPLETED BEFORE ANY BID IS CONSIDERED OR ACCEPTED OR ANY WORK IS PERFORMED:

1. Bidder's Name

2. Driver's License

3. State

4. Date of Birth

5. Social Security Number

6. Car License

7. Car Make and Model

8. Phone Number

9. Current Address

10. One reference: Name   Phone number

I HAVE READ THIS ENTIRE AGREEMENT AND AGREE TO ALL CONDITIONS. I UNDERSTAND AND WILL ABIDE BY THE RULES ABOVE.

I UNDERSTAND AND AGREE TO ALL PAY SCHEDULES, INSPECTION PROCEDURES, AND PENALTIES FOR LATE OR NON-COMPLETION.

I UNDERSTAND THAT I AM, ALONE, RESPONSIBLE FOR ALL TAXES, INSURANCE, AND LIABILITIES FOR MYSELF AND ANYONE I HIRE.

I WILL NOT HOLD *COMPANY* OR ANY PROPERTY OWNER RESPONSIBLE FOR ANY DAMAGES OR LIABILITIES ON THIS JOB.

I UNDERSTAND THAT I CANNOT PERFORM ANY WORK THAT IS NOT BID IN WRITING —AND ACCEPTED IN WRITING.

I UNDERSTAND THAT I CANNOT PERFORM ANY WORK UNTIL THIS AGREEMENT IS FILLED OUT COMPLETELY AND SIGNED.

THIS IS THE ONLY AGREEMENT BETWEEN MYSELF AND *COMPANY*—THERE ARE NO OTHERS—EITHER IMPLIED, ORAL, OR WRITTEN

Worker or Bidder

Date

INDEX